It's Not Me

40 Years as Director of
The Association of Banks in Singapore

It's Not Me

40 Years as Director of The Association of Banks in Singapore

Ong-Ang Ai Boon
with **Janice Tai**

NEW JERSEY • LONDON • SINGAPORE • BEIJING • SHANGHAI • HONG KONG • TAIPEI • CHENNAI • TOKYO

Published by

World Scientific Publishing Co. Pte. Ltd.
5 Toh Tuck Link, Singapore 596224
USA office: 27 Warren Street, Suite 401-402, Hackensack, NJ 07601
UK office: 57 Shelton Street, Covent Garden, London WC2H 9HE

British Library Cataloguing-in-Publication Data
A catalogue record for this book is available from the British Library.

Cover image courtesy of Layers Pte. Ltd.

IT'S NOT ME
40 Years as Director of The Association of Banks in Singapore

ISBN 978-981-127-875-4 (hardcover)
ISBN 978-981-127-897-6 (paperback)
ISBN 978-981-127-876-1 (ebook for institutions)
ISBN 978-981-127-877-8 (ebook for individuals)

For any available supplementary material, please visit
https://www.worldscientific.com/worldscibooks/10.1142/13481#t=suppl

Desk Editor: Lai Ann
Artist: Ng Chin Choon

Printed in Singapore

For my late husband, Hock Chye.

Thank you for your courage in proposing to walk away from our marriage.

Because of that, I died and was found by the One who gave me new life.

Totally in love with you, too.

Contents

Foreword

By Piyush Gupta, CEO, DBS Group

For everyone in Singapore's banking industry, Ai Boon has always been seen as a force of nature. This fantastic personal chronicle of her journey over fifty years, helming ABS while evolving "from tigress to cat", parallels the evolution of Singapore's financial landscape in the opposite direction — from cat to tiger! Through various anecdotes — cashless pay and ATM proliferation in the early 80s, launch of a code of conduct in the 90s, creating the credit bureau and so turning profitable at the turn of the century, the challenges with SIBOR in the global financial crisis, the creating of a world-class payments infrastructure and the world's largest fintech festival in the past decade — Ai Boon has vividly captured the context and priorities of the time, and ABS' and her own critical role in stewarding the industry to where it is today.

I worked with Ai Boon closely as ABS Chairman over two stints. I realised that from early days, she saw her and ABS' role not as an advocacy body but as an honest broker, keeping in mind the interests of multiple stakeholders, with the singular agenda of furthering Singapore's interests. Her sense of purpose has been defining, and comes through most vividly in this book. What also comes through is her own progression as a manager, a leader and a person. This book is not merely a chronicle of history, but a very readable story of challenges, faith and growth.

I recommend this book highly, whether to a financial services practitioner trying to understand the history of our industry, to the young person looking to shape a career, or to anyone seeking to understand the power of faith in producing extraordinary outcomes.

Foreword

By Sopnendu Mohanty, Chief Fintech Officer, MAS

I joined the MAS in August 2015 as an outsider from a global foreign bank and limited understanding of Singapore's ecosystem. As I was trying to ease into my new job, while simultaneously planning for a strategic global fintech seminar, I came to know of Ai Boon, who runs ABS, as an important stakeholder in Singapore banking.

When I first met her, I distinctly recall Ai Boon as the stereotypical senior person who was digital light in her thinking and more familiar with traditional financial services. But she had this "freak" willingness and rare responsiveness to engage in a topic which she was not completely comfortable with. She also had this little mysterious assuring smile, knowing she was getting herself into something exciting despite the unfamiliarity. I realised that I would be drawing out somebody who would experience a whole set of unknowns as we went forward.

We had lots of meetings after that, followed by several overseas roadshows together with our teams. Over many lunches and 'teh tariks',

I saw our many similarities — our willingness to take risks, and to believe in something one was not able to fully articulate yet.

We took the opportunity to discuss a wide range of topics which could be distilled into three common precepts. First, we both wanted to do things which would be impactful. Second, those things should be good for our community. And third, "Singapore first" — this 'motto' would always be at the back of our minds. And these goals would shape the projects we collaborated on.

The Singapore Fintech Festival (SFF) was a prime example. She put in much effort to understand what I was trying to do. Even as she was learning, her stake in the project grew as the number of registered participants rose exponentially, from the initial 1,000 people in total, to ultimately 13,000. All this despite having nothing in her hand where she could go to her stakeholders with firm numbers, projections and pay-offs. I think anybody in that situation, seeing the level of risk and commitment balloon that much, would have walked away. If Ai Boon had demurred, one of the most iconic successes of Singapore's fintech ecosystem — the Singapore FinTech Festival — would never have happened.

That lady didn't walk away.

The only reason she persevered with me was that there was something between us; something in me, something in her, that knew we could build unexpected things. It was as if there was somebody up there who was blessing this thing. And we just ran through that whole process with the sense that something would come out of it.

How significant has the SFF been for Singapore? Singapore's fintech growth rests on it in no small way, with annual fintech investments surging from US$20 million in 2014 to US$4 billion in 2022. The fintech ecosystem also created more than 20,000 jobs in Singapore. That is mind blowing.

The SFF is not a festival, in a sense. It is a global and strategic platform for convening people to reflect on how the industry has evolved, and the roles they play in this shift. It has also expanded its reach to host separate gatherings beyond Singapore, in Zurich, Switzerland, the PointZero Forum and in Kigali, Africa, the Inclusive Fintech Forum. Many countries have modelled their own fintech festival after Singapore's.

Almost every transformative digital project you pick in MAS, Ai Boon was involved: PayNow, SGQR, SGFinDex, Greenprint. Anything that requires our banking stakeholders to engage, Ai Boon steps in to support. She provides that intuitive role of a deft balancing act managing both industry stakeholders and MAS's strategic interest. That is a very difficult job because not every project will have apparent economic pay-offs for the stakeholders, especially those aimed at the collective good where economic incentives may not apply equally to everybody.

Consider PayNow. When she heard about this thing, she was taken by it, and proceeded to win over the banks to be part of the project. She went to her stakeholders and provided the project management, coordination, communication and media support. She was effective ; there is no other person I could think of who could have pulled it off. Today, ABS is the scheme owner of PayNow because no other stakeholder could see its potential at the time the concept was conceived. Now we are reaping the benefits of a highly scalable and successful payment enabler.

Now, practically everybody in this country can't live without PayNow. Annually, we are processing about $69 billion, from $10 billion in the first year on PayNow for individuals. On the corporate side, it started from only $2 billion transfers to now $55 billion transfers. Almost 6.5 million people are part of the PayNow mobile number and NRIC subscription. So this is not trivial: it's a vast infrastructure that needs a lot of process, policies, controls, possible issues, risk management.

Regardless, she was willing to bring stakeholders together to settle difficult and sensitive issues, such as operational gaps, operational risk management and stakeholder accountability. Ai Boon played that important role of ensuring that all the stakeholders were aligned for national projects. Anybody else in her place would have just walked out of it, with very logical reasoning.

You see the pattern now: each time, she was willing to take on a project even when she had no full understanding of it, or the extent of the impact, or the scale of the product. If she believed in someone's plans, she would look at ways to step in to help and then discover it would turn out to be a very big thing

Ai Boon and her team have played a critical role in supporting MAS connect PayNow to Thailand's PromptPay, to India's UPI and soon to Malaysia's DuitNow. Recently, Prime Minister Modi speaking on India's top 20 moments mentioned PayNow-UPI connectivity as one of those moments. It has got a profound global impact. G20 leaders at G20 India presidency meetings often cite PayNow-UPI connectivity as one of the global successes in the future of cross-border payments.

It's only people who have worked with Ai Boon closely in challenging conditions who can appreciate her contributions. Ai Boon brings an empathy-driven spirit, that is human, unrelenting, highly optimistic, partly driven by her own spiritual character, her faith and her inherent ability to look for goodness in every individual. Her natural instinct is not to find what the person is weak at; but to focus on what the person is good at. She will not indulge in your weaknesses, she will indulge in your strengths, or draw those out of you. She is faithful and persevering in seeking to do the right thing for Singapore and the community. That really drives her.

I was one of the dinner guests who had urged Ai Boon to write this book. The next generation should have an opportunity to understand her role in Singapore's financial sector success. If we don't document these things, we will lose a legacy of knowledge and practices which has made Singapore so successful.

What I hope that will come through from this book is her mindset of believing in people. An ambassador from Africa asked me: "Can we understand what Ai Boon does and replicate it in our country?" The next generation who wants to play her role in Singapore's development should know that there are crucial skill sets beyond what can be learnt from academic books. This book is a complement to an academic book; I can go to a college, take an advanced management degree, but I need this 'Ai Boon playbook' along with that.

So what exactly is her secret?

To me, her spiritual brain overrides her logical brain. If you were to use a trained brain, you can't do all these things. Your trained brain will say this is not possible. Your spiritual brain will say it is possible.

It is her faith that sees things and people as inherently good, and that if she sticks to it, ultimately the outcome will be good. It may not be visible or obvious initially, but it can only be discovered at the end. And till the end, one may still not be completely sure. The person who can hold on to that belief for months and months is what we need, and that is Ai Boon.

How This Book Came About

The book that you are holding in your hands now nearly did not come into being.

Over the years, many friends and colleagues have pushed and prodded me to write a book.

"You are a good storyteller," I was told. They wanted me to share all my experiences which had encouraged them since I became a Christian four decades ago, including how I overcame difficult situations in my personal and professional life with the insights and solutions that were divinely inspired.

In particular, they wanted to know how the former me — a tigress — could be tamed to become a cat, with my broken marriage restored and office tensions defused in the process.

Others in banking circles know that I have had a front-row seat to many key changes and events in the industry, having served in it for more than half a century since 1969. They wanted the insider 'scoop' on the many untold and behind-the-scenes stories within an industry that has grown to be a significant contributor to our country's Gross Domestic Product (GDP).

All these requests were heard but had fallen on deaf ears until an eventful evening at the Singapore FinTech Festival Appreciation Dinner at Marina Bay Sands in November 2021. Due to COVID-19 restrictions, we were seated at a table of five.

While eating the entrée of seafood and salad, Mr Navin Suri, the Chief Executive Officer of Percipient with whom I had worked closely on several FinTech industry events, leaned over from my left side and earnestly suggested: "Ai Boon, you should write a book about the values that The Association of Banks in Singapore (ABS) has been guided by under your helm. It is a trusted organisation that represents the banking industry and enjoys good rapport with the Monetary Authority of Singapore (MAS)."

His trailing voice was immediately echoed by Mr Sopnendu Mohanty, currently the Chief FinTech Officer at MAS, who was seated on my right. "Yes, you should write the book and we can launch it at the FinTech Festival in November 2022!"

Throughout the rest of the night, the other two guests at the table also chimed in to persuade me to write a book. As we finished dessert, MAS' Managing Director, Mr Ravi Menon, came by the table to thank ABS and me for organising the dinner. Upon learning that the group had been urging me to write a book on ABS, he was quick to support the idea and emphatically said: "Yes, do it!"

These comments reminded me of all the encouragement I had

received from others through the years. I knew ABS' golden 50th anniversary was coming up soon and such a key milestone finally ignited within me a nagging need to write a book to share more about my life's work at ABS.

Yet there was also a strong resistance to focus on how 'Ong Ai Boon' had successfully led the organisation for four decades. I was absolutely allergic to any suggestion that I had done it, as I know that all the work could only have been done by the amazing grace of God. It was not simply serendipity — it was the favour of God that had led me to build up an effective Secretariat which has not only been successful in its execution of projects, but also in earning the trust and respect of its Chairmen, the Council members, the regulators and stakeholders in Singapore and the ASEAN region through the years.

If the book were to be launched in November 2022, we would have had a rather tight deadline as the writing had to be completed by September in time for the printing to be done.

Thus, I approached the current ABS Chairman, Mr Wee Ee Cheong (Deputy Chairman and CEO of United Overseas Bank), and expressed my intention to publish a book. He, too, quickly endorsed the idea as he felt the book would help the public have a better appreciation of ABS' role in the banking industry and the wider financial sector. It would offer insights into the workings of the Association and how it fosters collaboration and partnership between industry players and the Government.

As time was of the essence, the authors were promptly identified to work on a narrative that would highlight the Association's role in the banking industry and how it has become a trusted and respected industry voice when engaging with MAS and other stakeholders.

I was also cognisant of the fact that the Association would not have been this successful in its contributions to the development of Singapore as an international financial centre if it had not been for several factors.

There was the competent leadership that came with a stable government and civil service, a strong moral system laid down by Singapore's first Prime Minister Mr Lee Kuan Yew as well as a prescient and trusted regulator: MAS.

Within ABS, the leadership of the Chairman of the Association which rotates among the three local banks — Development Bank of Singapore (DBS), Oversea-Chinese Banking Corporation (OCBC) and United Overseas Bank (UOB) — is vital. The Chairman bank provides overall direction for the Association, and also resources ABS' work by providing most of the leads for the ABS committees and taskforces, and industry representation for external engagements.

The ABS management also includes the 18 Council members that guide and shape its policies and decisions, which are in turn executed by the Secretariat. ABS' continual relevance and success is also only made possible with the expertise and commercial knowledge of the various Standing Committees, Workgroup Chairmen and committee members from our member banks.

Although I was aware of the contributions I had made to the effective management of the ABS Secretariat through the decades, I was uncomfortable with telling ABS' story as though it was due to my own ability or personality. If my contributions were to be highlighted, they needed to give credit to God Himself. However, as the book at that time was to be secular, so as to reach the business community and beyond, then my role in ABS had to be downplayed. I belaboured this point to the writers on several occasions.

Throughout the first seven months of meetings and interviews done for the upcoming book, I had sleepless nights agonising over its content. I knew the book was not to be a historical record of corporate events that had happened in ABS, but it had to tell the full story of the success and effectiveness of the work of the Association. To do this, however, credit would need to be given not only to the external circumstantial factors but also to the grace of God in guiding me. But this was not possible given the book's secular framework. As I was unable to unravel these contradictions within myself, it became a very vexing period for me.

Even as I struggled emotionally with this tension, the book continued to be written, and soon, the first draft of the book with 12 chapters was done by August 2022.

The draft was well researched and deftly written, with input from fresh interviews with the ABS Chairmen, former MAS officers and other people who have worked with ABS. It turned out to be a historical compilation of the key works of the Association from inception to the present, which may have no present currency and would not attract readership. While the facts were true, the draft did not tell the complete story. It did not do justice to the rich reality that I have experienced first-hand when working with the relevant people on various projects.

Without writing much about me managing the ABS Secretariat, as the writers were instructed, the most important person behind how the Association came to shake off its 'sleepy hollow' image to be the vibrant and successful organisation that it is today was inevitably left out. And that person is not me. It's God!

I prayed and sought wisdom from God regarding the book, and He told me to tell of the work that He had done through me during the time that I am in ABS, so that if any boasting is to be done, it would be to "boast in the Lord".

In the wee hours of the morning of 23 September 2022, God prompted me to turn to my Bible and seek out Proverbs Chapter 23 (in alignment to the date that day). As I read it, verse 23 jumped out at me: "Buy the truth and do not sell it; also wisdom and instruction and understanding."

With this conviction, I was given the courage to can the first draft. I had given the authors the wrong brief. I explained and apologised to them for my error in judgement in relation to my perceived expectations of the readers. A new author was then sought out to do a total re-write of this book.

Now, the book certainly could not be launched in November 2022 at the Singapore FinTech Festival as was originally intended. It would now be launched at the Association's 50th Anniversary celebration during its Annual General Meeting (AGM) dinner in June 2023 instead.

After all, I would also be celebrating my "50 years in ABS" — it was the first 10 years of developmental work that I did at MAS that trained me for these 40 years of managing the ABS Secretariat.

This book might have cost twice of what it should have, on top of having its publication delayed, but I do not regret having it rewritten and delayed in order to obey God and follow my conscience. As Navin Suri, one of the two proponents for the book — and a successful fintech entrepreneur himself — quipped: "It's okay. Writing a book is like launching a start-up, and all fintech start-ups have to burn cash!"

This book is a personal account of more than half a century of my time in the banking industry — especially in ABS — that was primarily influenced by my being a disciple of Jesus Christ since 1983. That was the year when my late husband, Ong Hock Chye, issued me an ultimatum: "I can't live with you anymore. If things don't change, let's separate. You can take the house and we each go our own way." I was such a bad-tempered and workaholic wife that he had decided to walk out of our marriage.

The book will also trace the irony of how I did not choose to work in ABS at the beginning, though I have been serving the Association as its Director for four decades. Yet because of God's plans and His hand in my life, my time with ABS has been purposeful, enjoyable and enriching. By God's grace, I still hope to work till I am 95.

To know Ai Boon is to know the meaning of "rare" up close. She is a leader who not only created, but for 40 straight years, continues to lead the iconic Association of Banks in Singapore.

Her innate hospitable nature violently contrasts with her deeply resented, my-way-or-the-highway leadership style. And her self-taught transformation from a loud, argumentative firebrand to a faith-led believer and healer for all, is just as rare.

Fearlessness remains her biggest asset, which she generously brings to every page in the book, openly talking about things personal and professional, with only God to answer to. Her autobiography is as rare a gem as she is, with countless usable lessons on professional leadership, finding purpose and self-healing.

Navin Suri
CEO, Percipient

Prologue

I will be 77 years old this year.

Looking back, I have spent more than half my life working in the banking sector since I graduated in 1969.

As I reflect on how the years have gone by, I see how God has been faithful in answering the one and only question I had struggled to find an answer to in my younger days.

I was 36 years old then and had all the trappings of a good life: A landed home, three cars, good investments, club memberships, a helper, a driver and three children. I had also been appointed to helm ABS the year before.

But, for some reason, there was no contentment in me. Instead, I harboured a lot of anger and my hot-tempered self took it out on the people around me.

Twelve years into our marriage, when my husband told me he could not live with me any longer and intended to walk out on our marriage, my world collapsed.

Firstly, I knew I needed to have my marriage fixed in order to keep my family intact. Secondly, I wanted better relationships with others. Thirdly, I also desired to end well spiritually and be in paradise when I die.

The other faiths and world philosophies that I explored could not help me.

I began to realise that what I was actually seeking, beyond those three areas of priority, was the most fundamental question of our human existence: What is the meaning of my life?

It was the Christian God who heard and answered the deepest cry of my heart.

Little did I know that He had already lovingly planned and chosen a purpose for me, even before I knew Him, just as it is written in Ephesians 2:10.

As I trace the many forks in the crossroads of life where I could have meandered and gone on entirely different paths, I can see now that the path that He has led me on is indeed the best.

I see His fingerprints all over the story of my life, even from my younger days.

When I was young, I excelled in the humanities, especially subjects such as geography. But I was ambitious and did not want to land up in the teaching profession or civil service.

So, I took economics instead, though it was not my strong suit at all. It would give me better chances in life, I reckoned, and I was attracted by the banking sector.

Upon my graduation, I joined Chung Khiaw Bank in 1969. It was taken over by the United Overseas Bank in 1971. My husband later applied to join Citibank, after he served National Service following his graduation from the University of Singapore, but its bank policy then stipulated that spouses of their employees could not work in the same industry.

For the sake of my husband, I left Chung Khiaw Bank in 1972 and joined the regulator Monetary Authority of Singapore (MAS) instead. MAS began operations in 1971, with its key focus being to oversee Singapore's financial system and manage its reserves, as the de facto central bank. Since 2002, MAS has also assumed the function of currency issuance. To ensure the long-term development of the economy, Singapore would need the banking and financial services sector to play a prominent role in driving high value-added activities.

I spent a fulfilling decade at MAS undertaking several major developmental policies. Yet the hand of God, seen through shifting life circumstances, was at work once again.

When then Deputy Prime Minister of Singapore and Minister for Education, Dr Goh Keng Swee, took over as Chairman of MAS in 1980, he initiated a major restructuring in MAS. After numerous interviews, many of my colleagues were axed and shown the door. I survived the 'bloodbath' and, by default through the process of elimination, rose up to be the number two in charge of my department. Those were big shoes to fill and I did not think I had what it took for such a huge responsibility, so I looked for a way out. Perhaps I could go to a stockbroking firm, I thought.

However, during this time, then ABS Chairman Mr Chua Kim Yeow, who was also President of DBS, approached me to take up the top executive post in ABS. I declined, not wanting to join such a 'sleepy hollow'. Chua pursued me with the offer by going through my husband, who urged me to take up the job to get Chua off his back.

Once again, I thought I would do my husband a favour and check out the Association by tagging along when a Singapore delegation made a work trip to Kuala Lumpur for the ASEAN Banking Conference in 1982. I wanted to observe its team at work and see if its work interested me.

An overeager reporter got wind of the news, assumed that I had formally joined ABS, and published an article in *The Straits Times* that I had accepted the top post at ABS while I was in the Malaysian capital.

In some sense, that news announcement sealed my fate. I had not officially said "yes", but was not averse to it. I went with the flow, not knowing that therein laid God's purposes for my life.

Over the next four decades, God would use ABS as my furnace for shaping and transforming me to be more like Him.

There were many difficult moments and I was so overwhelmed during those times that I almost left my job four times over. But God intervened and gave me the grace and wisdom to sustain me.

Over the years, ABS has represented the interests of the banking industry effectively and, alongside the banks and MAS, facilitated the development of Singapore as a financial centre. It has championed many key projects that have benefitted the people of the nation. These include building up a financially enlightened population, enabling the responsible provision of personal credit with the establishment of Credit Bureau Singapore and providing greater convenience to consumers through PayNow.

ABS has been a one-stop shop for banking and industry matters, whether it is receiving overseas delegations, organising golf tournaments, or fostering relationships with our neighbours in the region through its role in the ASEAN Bankers Association and the Dr Goh Keng Swee Scholarship.

From having accumulated hundreds of thousands of dollars in the red initially to eventually having a surplus of over $10 million, ABS has turned the corner and used some of these resources to help fund financial programmes for the private sector and the community.

ABS is celebrating its 50th anniversary this year. Looking back, I see that all the achievements and milestones of the Association are due to God's gracious orchestration of situations and people.

I am thankful that God has chosen me, and equipped me with a particular set of giftings to play a small part in all of these.

I have found the meaning of my life — knowing my Creator, having the guarantee of eternal life and fulfilling His purposes for me to love and serve others around me — whether it is at work, at home or elsewhere.

Beyond myself, it is also clear to me that God's hand is on Singapore. Singapore has a call and destiny for her to be the Antioch of Asia, as Billy Graham prophesied to the nation in 1978. Therefore, God has blessed her with astute economic vision and the capacity to engage in high value-added activities.

My hope is that Singapore will remain upright and effect justice with integrity, so that it will continue to succeed as a reputable and effective financial centre. Only with such a foundation will ABS also remain a respected, credible and trusted voice of the industry that supports the work of an ever-expanding and dynamic international financial centre.

As for me, my work at ABS carries on. I will not leave a day sooner if His will is for me to remain, and neither will I stay a day longer if He tells me to leave.

Part 1

A Dramatic Start

I have known Ai Boon as the Director of ABS since I joined the MAS in 1986. It is no exaggeration to say that she is an icon of the banking industry. As ABS Director, she is instrumental in the constructive partnerships that many stakeholders have with banks in Singapore, and one of the key "go-to persons" for me and my colleagues at MAS.

With Ai Boon helming the ABS Secretariat, we can always count on her support, feedback and inputs. Her energy and can-do spirit are infectious, and she is not coy to express any concerns affecting banks or their customers. Ai Boon has been at the centre of many key initiatives of ABS. A few examples include the work many years ago with Singapore Foreign Exchange Market Committee (SFEMC) on settlement of outstanding MYR transactions following exchange controls in Malaysia in 1998, or more regular initiatives such as the industry stress test exercises; to the more recent work to co-ordinate the implementation of the regulations to reduce consumer indebtedness to 12 times their monthly income, broad Covid-related measures, security of digital banking, and guidelines on sustainable practices and countless other initiatives.

Ai Boon is a woman of all seasons. She can be fun-loving, lively and super charming in ABS social events yet thoughtful, focused and determined in seeing through projects and initiatives as decided by the ABS Council. I am told that she is very meticulous on tasks and can be demanding on deadlines but I am sure the 'tough love' is also appreciated by all. ABS' role and relevance owe much to her charisma and chemistry with everyone around her.

On a more personal note, Ai Boon has become a good friend over the years. We kept in touch on several occasions even after I left the Authority. Her religious faith and positive outlook on life are uplifting to colleagues, friends and family. I am sure this book will be an inspiration to many of us.

Ong Chong Tee
Former Deputy MD, MAS

Chapter 1

The Fait Accompli

It was nothing short of a fait accompli.

"MAS official gets top post at bank association" read the news headline of an article published in *The Straits Times* on 11 February 1982.

The truth was that the MAS official in question — yours truly — had not officially said "yes" to taking up the top executive post in ABS when the article ran.

Yet it seemed a done deal, and that was how I joined the organisation and would eventually go on to head it for the next 40 odd years.

I did not object to the decision that was made for me. Sometimes in life, you feel that good decisions have been made and you don't have to worry about them. So, I actually went with the flow.

Even though I will be 77 years old this year, leading the Association still fills me with much passion.

ABS is an organisation that represents the interests of over 150 local and foreign banks in the financial industry, and works with regulators, consumers and other stakeholders to establish a sound banking structure for Singapore. It was first set up in 1973.

Over the years, the Association has played a key role in supporting the nation's transformation to become a world-renowned international financial centre — from a very small domestic finance and banking industry, we have grown to be a large international banking centre.

A Call and a Newspaper Article

Yet few know that I had begun my leadership journey at ABS reluctantly, at least initially.

When I was first approached to take up the post in late 1981, I demurred.

"Why would I want to join a 'sleepy hollow'" was my immediate retort to the offer.

By then, I had been with the MAS for almost 10 years, and had been exposed to various significant developments in its nascent role as a central bank, regulator and policymaker.

Back then, the Asian Dollar Market was just established and it was a tremendous experience for me to work with policymakers in the licensing of new banks and financial institutions, and in the development of the offshore market through the promotion and drafting of tax incentives in the MAS division which I headed.

In contrast, ABS seemed to me a nondescript association, only known for setting interest rates for bank deposits, as well as forex rates, commissions and fees for bank services.

But the Association found another way to get through to me, this time via my husband.

"Ling, can you please take up the post at ABS and get Mr Chua Kim Yeow off my back?" My husband pleaded with me over the phone.

It turned out that then ABS Chairman Chua Kim Yeow, who was also President of DBS, had called my husband, then OCBC's Deputy General Manager. Mr Chua had repeated the job offer, and my husband conveyed the message to me.

At that time, I was heading the Foreign Division in the Banking and Financial Institution Department of MAS. Coincidentally, I was also looking to leave MAS following an internal consolidation exercise done in 1981. In a bid to revamp MAS then, former Minister and Chairman of MAS Dr Goh Keng Swee and his team had interviewed all existing staff and had axed around 40 per cent of them.

As a result of the exercise, I inadvertently became the number two in the department and had to report to Dr Goh and other ministers directly.

It was too stressful for me without having the 'cover' of senior management officials above me that I used to have, and I was ready to leave.

While I had been planning to leave MAS for a new challenge, it would have been to a more exciting stockbroking job rather than the low-profile Association.

Yet at my husband's urging, I felt obliged to respond to the job offer.

I told Mr Chua that I would consider the post and see if the Association would be a right fit by first doing a recce trip.

Thus, I flew to Kuala Lumpur with the ABS delegation to join the ASEAN Banking Conference in February 1982, though I had not yet formally joined the Association. The conference was hosted by The Association of Banks in Malaysia.

While I was in the Malaysian capital, *The Straits Times* published the article that I had accepted the top post at ABS.

My husband immediately called me with news of the article.

I was surprised but went along with it. During the conference, I met many CEOs and realised that ABS had its own networks and role to play in the regional banking industry as well. (Indeed, groupings like the ASEAN Bankers Association would come to play an important role in the work of ABS, as relationships between bank CEOs are forged over conferences, regional projects and social events.) So, I was not averse to joining ABS.

On my return to Singapore, I accepted the offer. It ended the Association's eight-month search for its Director-General, a newly created position as it was forming a permanent secretariat for the first time after being set up nine years prior in 1973.

At the MAS exit interview, I was pleased that then Deputy Managing Director Mr Lim Kim San complimented me on the move to head up the Association. He told me that I had found "a niche" for myself. This was a strong endorsement as Mr Lim was then one of the key pillars in the Government, having served as a Minister in various ministries.

Shortly after I joined ABS in April 1982, I also met UOB's Chairman,

Dr Wee Cho Yaw, at the Association's annual general meeting in June and he remarked: "They found the right person for the job."

These endorsements by the two doyens of the political and banking industry in Singapore assured me that I had made the right career move.

While their confidence in me was reassuring, the move from MAS to ABS was initially a culture shock.

As I was new to helming an organisation, it was the first time I had to oversee other functions and build a team from scratch. Back then, our team consisted only of four staff: myself and three others who had been seconded from OCBC. Of the four included Ms Ng Soo Moi, the accountant, who continued to work with me for 30 years until she retired in 2013, and Mr Osman Shariff, the despatch staff, for 27 years until he retired in 2007.

I had to run an office which I had never done before — employ people, pay salaries, decide on human resources policies and help to oversee the accounts. This was all new to me. I was an absolute rookie.

The other challenge was to convince bankers that working with ABS would be good for the industry. The Association does not have the clout of MAS, the central bank.

When I was with MAS, each time I called up banks, they would sit up, drop everything and come if I asked. But when I joined ABS, it was a humbling process. It was hard to get bankers to come for Committee meetings initially, and I recall an instance when a committee member, who had been appointed by his CEO for a project, told me off when we were working on an issue by saying: "Why, we are here only to help *you* do *your* work."

I quickly realised the need to build up credibility, standing, respect and goodwill from the people that I would be working with. I could not rely on the authority of the MAS badge anymore.

Fortunately, my decade of work with MAS had exposed me to development work and deepened my understanding of policies. It also left me with an invaluable network among the relevant government agencies that would prove useful for my work in ABS.

Another delightful and significant takeaway for me during my time at MAS was the experience of working with Mrs Elizabeth Sam, then Chief Manager, and second only to the Managing Director of MAS, Mr Michael Wong Pakshong. She played a key role in the growth of Singapore as a financial centre, and in particular the development of the Asian Dollar Market and the foreign exchange market.

Still new to the working world then, I was struck by how Mrs Sam was always elegantly dressed. She came to work in beautiful gowns with coordinated jewelry. Yet her stylish image belied her professionalism as a top career woman whose competence and strong negotiating skills regularly disarmed suave bankers and rugged rubber brokers alike.

I was so impressed with her beauty and brains that, when I was interviewed by a newspaper reporter on inspiring women leaders for a follow-up on the paper's article on the hit 1990s TV character Murphy Brown, I naturally pointed to her. In my heart of hearts, I wanted to be like her — supremely poised and competent for the job at hand, while retaining every ounce of her femininity.

ABS grew and developed slowly at its own pace. I had the freedom to manage ABS without close supervision from the Chairman or Council, although I could always look to the ABS Chairman, whom I reported to, for guidance. The Council was performance and outcome-oriented, which sat well with me.

Championing Change, Consultation and Collaboration

While ABS is breaking boundaries today, the non-profit organisation began because of a break-up. It was formed in 1973 after a currency split between Singapore and Malaysia. This led to the separation of the banking association which was then called The Association of Banks of Malaysia and Singapore (ABMS).

But it was only when a permanent ABS Secretariat was formed in 1981 that ABS began to resemble its current form.

Shortly before I joined ABS, there were two key changes. One, ABS Chairmanship would no longer be retained with OCBC (which was the Chairman Bank for nine years following the split), but rotated every two years among the then four larger local banks — DBS, OCBC, Overseas Union Bank (OUB) and UOB. (This was reduced to three local banks after UOB took over OUB in 2002). Two, the Secretariat had to be restructured with a permanent team that was funded by its members. This would provide continuity with a rotating Chairmanship, as the financial landscape was becoming more complex. The secretariat work was previously undertaken by a team seconded from OCBC.

DBS was voted by the members to be the first Chairman Bank of the new permanent Secretariat at ABS starting from May 1981, with then DBS President Mr Chua Kim Yeow assuming the role of the

Chairman of ABS. They then searched for the new Director-General of ABS, which led to Mr Chua headhunting me over. When I came on board in 1982, I dropped the term 'General' from the title, as it seemed too formal and pompous.

Over time, with the liberalisation of the financial sector in Singapore, the banking industry shed its cartel of interest and fee setting to permit freer competition of rates. As more and more foreign banks and financial institutions were admitted, the membership of ABS also grew from its initial grouping of about 80 members.

ABS did not involve itself in the banks' commercial business, but focused on working with its members to provide bye-laws, codes and guidelines in setting standards for banks' operations, as well as building up the reputation and quality of their services to customers.

When I became its Director, I brought my MAS-influenced brand of organisation to ABS.

I set up the registry to be like the MAS registry, whether it was the filing system or the file colour. I also sought to instil more professionalism and decorum in the Association by ensuring that the Council members wear suits to meetings. The seniority of the Council representation is sustained, as only the CEO and his/her designated alternate may attend the Council meetings. That's how my persona rubbed off onto ABS.

Our job was to ensure that all ABS' codes and guidelines were complied with. If any member bank was found deviating from any of the guidelines, the bank would be duly alerted so that they could immediately make rectifications.

For the last 40 years, I anchored ABS with a simple dictum: To do what is right for Singapore's financial centre and be the 'honest broker' among the banks as well as between MAS and the banks.

The role of ABS, I soon realised, went beyond the initial mandate of looking after the interests of the banking fraternity in Singapore. It also had to consider the national interests of Singapore, and be the connector, or even mediator, between the Government and the banks, in order to balance the needs of all parties in the Republic's quest to be the next international financial centre of choice.

The Association has a close and unique partnership with the central bank and financial regulator MAS. I tried to be the glue that gels everything together, creating the stickiness and trust between the public and private sectors. Working with the banks, my team and I regularly submitted proposals and feedback to the MAS on the operational aspects of banking to influence its regulatory policies.

These policies sought to enhance Singapore's competitiveness and attract businesses to our shores. My previous experience in MAS came in handy, as it gave me a better understanding of MAS' policy considerations, and I would take them into account in our submissions.

Balancing the Needs of All Parties

Everyone wanted to get to the same destination, but the journey was more uncertain.

Push the pace of opening up the banking sector too quickly, and the banks could recoil in fear of intense competition. Go too slowly, and Singapore could lose the race. The views of local banks, with their different sizes, market interests and customer focus, were also not always in sync, with ABS squeezed in between diverse and conflicting positions.

It wasn't an easy role to play. While policy setting was the Government's remit, ABS' role was to gather the industry players into committees and taskforces to work out how to implement the policy or project. Given the rich diversity of our members, there would naturally be a panoply of ideas on what should be the industry standard. Given market competition, individual banks would also seek to protect their own interests in these industry initiatives.

In such circumstances, I would have to play the role of referee-cum-counsellor and go between the various parties to persuade them to work towards a more balanced outcome for the greater good. This was a role no individual bank could play; only ABS could fulfil this role effectively, being a neutral party with no commercial interests to advance or defend.

"Don't blunt the knife," I would sometimes warn the banks, when discussions veered towards watering down the burden of compliance on banks whenever we drew up the implementation guidelines and standards. For the Association to be a credible and effective voice for the industry, our standards and guidelines had to be fair, transparent and practical.

Then there were critical situations when the Chairman had to step in personally. During the global rate-rigging probe that spread to the Singapore Interbank Offered Rate (SIBOR) in 2013, DBS happened to be the ABS Chairman that year. Mr Piyush Gupta, DBS' CEO, directly led many intense discussions among his banking peers.

Six years later, in line with global interest rate benchmark reforms, Singapore began its interest rate transition, replacing both the SIBOR and Swap Offer Rate (SOR) with the Singapore Overnight Rate Average (SORA), a massive undertaking spanning several years and affecting almost every part of the financial sector. The ABS Chairmanship had just rotated to OCBC and Mr Samuel Tsien, the bank's CEO, together with MAS, personally helmed an extensive steering committee that has thus far managed to steer the industry through a smooth transition.

During the pandemic, CEOs of the major banks met weekly with MAS to discuss how the industry could offer financial support to impacted households and companies as the crisis unfolded.

ABS thus functions as an honest broker. On the one hand, it offers MAS consolidated and constructive feedback from the banks on financial policies. On the other hand, ABS conducts seminars to convey the Government's position to member banks, brings the banks together to work out implementation details for the policies and organises workshops to familiarise the banks with industry standards or guidelines.

It is a fine balance. The job requires the intricate skill of diplomacy, for which I have a natural flair — especially with food diplomacy. It is very hard to be angry or upset with a person with whom you have shared a good meal. That is why my team and I never fail to feed our guests at every appointment or meeting, whether it was with luxurious black pearl durian, mango sticky rice dessert from the best Thai restaurant in town or a *nasi padang* feast from the most hidden gem of a stall tucked away in an industrial estate.

While food is important in the ABS approach of winning friends and calming foes, it was not always applicable. Not if you need the entire working population to migrate from receiving their salaries in envelopes of cash, or literal pay packets, to having the money withdrawn from a new banking machine — the ATM.

One of my most vivid early memories of ABS' work was during the Government's push for a "Cashless Payday" in 1984, a campaign to get people to open bank accounts so that they could receive their salaries electronically from their employers, and to use the ATMs whenever they needed cash.

Back in those days, this was a huge change. In the past, employers would need to inform their bank every month of the amount of cash they would be withdrawing for the salaries of their employees. They would then prepare the individual pay packets for their workers, who would go straight to the bank to deposit the money after receiving it.

It was a highly manual process that created operational 'logjams' every month, and one vulnerable to criminal interception. ABS then had to educate companies to stagger their collections, and to take precautions against robbers eyeing the substantial prize at hand. It was not uncommon for companies to lose the salaries that they had just collected as they were being stalked. Some were robbed once they stepped out of the bank; others had their cars broken into when they left the monies in the car while they went for lunch.

In those days, financial crime was a physical affair. ABS issued guidelines requiring bank tellers to operate behind bars, and prohibited sunglasses and helmets from being worn in the banking halls. We also organised training courses for frontline staff on what they should do if they were to find themselves in an armed robbery situation.

The introduction of ATMs was thus a big transition for society, with users needing a unique Personal Identification Number (PIN) to withdraw cash. Banking habits had to change and customers needed to be acquainted with the new technology. ABS produced a 12-minute video to educate people on how to use the ATM. For the video, I got my traditional *samfoo*-wearing mother-in-law, representing the older generation, to act as a bank customer. It showed her going to the ATM to withdraw money while on the way to the market.

There was also the initial confusion over the need to use a PIN when using the ATM card at the ATM machine. Some were afraid they would forget their PIN numbers and proceeded to write them down on the back of the cards — meaning anyone who got hold of the card could withdraw the person's money.

ABS had to raise awareness on the matter and tell the public: "It is like a cheque; if you actually put your PIN number on the ATM card, it is like giving them a blank cheque with your signature on it."

With this project, ABS also took on the new role of promoting the Government's policies to bank consumers. The banks would individually do their own customised marketing. But ABS, as an industry representative, would promote the ATMs.

There were more of these campaigns to come — from the National Productivity Campaign to the National Courtesy Campaign, to solving the skilled manpower shortage in banks as well as supporting the nation's drive towards digital payment look-up systems such as PayNow.

As the role of ABS gradually evolved, one thing was constant: We could not lose sight of the national agenda for Singapore to develop into a global financial hub. While the Association had a close partnership with MAS and other relevant government ministries, it also sought to support the banks and consumers on the ride towards a first-world economy.

Seeking Perfection or Craving Acceptance?

Work was fulfilling for me. I enjoyed the work immensely because my performance-oriented self could see visible results for the efforts I put into it.

It was an exciting time, in the earlier years, when banks were coming into Singapore and I received many an invitation to cocktail nights that celebrated their entries. Though I had three young children then, I found myself attending up to two cocktails a night.

While I threw myself into work, my seniors and colleagues found me difficult to work with. I had a mind of my own and was often argumentative, even with the ABS Chairmen who were above me. I did things according to what I felt should be done, despite receiving differing views and objections from others.

"Ai Boon, you are so peremptory," said the former *Business Times* Editor Ms Tan Sai Siong when I worked with her on a project.

My "peremptory" nature — meaning one that issued instructions brusquely, expecting to be obeyed immediately with no questions asked — was well-known in the office.

Whenever others could not understand my point of view or instructions, or when I was faced with rejections that I could not ignore, I would become so frustrated that I would lash out in anger and harsh words.

Some assumed it was due to my perfectionistic streak, but I later realised that I was simply searching for and craving acceptance.

I was not consciously aware of it then, but found out later on that each disagreement triggered me because it made me feel rejected. I hated to be misunderstood or rejected because that was how my mother had made me feel from a young age. She had not accepted me for who I was.

Such explosions of anger and frustration in the office inevitably bubbled over to the home front.

"Mum, why are you always angry with us when you come home?" My then six-year-old younger son, Tze Ru, asked me one day at dinner time. Even my children noticed my volatile moods and explosive moments.

Relations with my husband were no better. Though married, we both continued living our own lives like singles. Heated disagreements often broke out whenever we interacted. I acted out so unreasonably that I could argue until I manoeuvred a wrong into a right.

After a particularly heated argument one day, my gentle giant of a husband blurted out: "I have given you everything you want, but you are not happy. What else do you want?"

"I don't know," I replied. "I need to know the meaning of life."

I was shocked at what I had just said.

Yet it also made sense. I was then 36 years old and had all the trappings of a good life: A landed home, three cars, good investments, club memberships, a domestic helper and driver, and three children.

But, for some reason, I was not happy and did not like myself. I was an angry and quick-tempered person who frequently took out my unhappiness on the people around me.

The stress that I faced at work and at home took a toll on my health. I had sleepless nights and days when I could not function due to migraines and vertigo which persisted and continued to intensify. At night, I would take strong painkillers which doubled up as my sleeping pills. In the day, I would pop other medications and supplements to help me stay awake and have the energy I needed to get through another day.

There was no peace in my life, and my husband felt it, too.

Chapter 2

The Ultimatum

In the middle of a day in 1983, my husband walked up to me and said: "I can't live with you any longer. Let's separate. You can take the house and we each go our own way."

For once in a very long time, I had no words.

I did not expect it, but I was not surprised at his proposal to separate, either.

I knew I was at fault and, by then, I was already trying to seek help for myself. I had turned to various management theories and gurus to try and fix myself.

On my office desk, for instance, were cue cards laid out all over as reminders: "Don't shout", "Stay calm", "Stay cool".

I also sought out various faiths and philosophies to assuage the emptiness I felt within myself. Deep down, I wanted to find the meaning of life.

Since young, I have been a spiritual person. Friends would come to me to have their palms read or to check the *fengshui* of a house as my intuition often led me to make uncannily astute assessments. I also dabbled in occult practices such as consulting astrologers and fortune tellers.

Turning to all these did not give me the meaning or peace that I needed. Though I put up a tough exterior, I was struggling with low self-esteem, insecurity and self-condemnation.

Aware that I was not well-received at work and at home, rejection was a major sore point for me.

So my husband's proposal for separation was, to me, the ultimate rejection.

God knew how to break me. If my husband had left me, I would have gone mad or died.

People often refer to me and my feisty spirit; as I would always say in Teochew: *bui si gai* ("cannot die"). This ultimate rejection from my own husband was necessary for me to be broken in, so that I could become contrite. It takes different experiences for each of us to reach that place of brokenness.

Desperate to know how to work on myself and find meaning to life, I went down the rabbit hole in search of answers.

I wrote copiously in my journal that I was determined to change, and sought out various faiths, philosophies, idols and even self-help courses.

But no management guru nor talisman worked.

Instead, a series of events that unfolded unexpectedly provided the answers I was seeking.

Three Dreams

It started when a close friend of mine came down with a debilitating liver disease. Dr Timothy Seow, the late renowned Singaporean architect, was known for pioneering the "bungalows in the air" concept for apartments.

In the past, we were part of a group of friends who would take turns to host parties. Eating, drinking and merrymaking were often the order of the day.

Despite initially languishing from the disease, he later received the healing touch of God and was miraculously healed in 1982. He came away from the experience talking non-stop about God, bubbling over with joy.

Under his influence, our group of friends, including myself, began gathering at his house for home meetings instead of raucous partying.

At that time, I also happened to hear the testimony of Rev Dr Neville Tan, one of the most feared and wanted criminals in Singapore. He was jailed many times for various crimes, including involvement in a gang-related murder.

But God met him in prison and his life took a radical turn. He studied for a doctorate while behind bars and eventually became a pastor and evangelist.

I was very taken by Rev Neville's story because the nature of the God whom he met in prison intrigued me.

It struck me that Rev Neville did not have to do anything, be it good works or sacrifices, to meet this God. In fact, it was God who chose to meet him in prison, the very place where he could not do or offer anything.

The grace and mercy of Rev Neville's God appealed to me because I was brought up believing that I needed to do good works to earn favour in order to secure a better afterlife.

Thus, I grew up internalising the fear of punishment, often worrying about whether I would end up in any of the 18 levels of hell. So, I adhered to certain superstitions rigidly, such as not allowing my husband to go to work if it was his birthday or whenever there was a funeral to attend.

Once, I reminded my older brother to make sure that he burnt enough offerings after my death, so that I would have a better afterlife. In jest, he asked me to pass him the money needed to pay for the offerings and the chanting. I had witnessed the need for all these at my father's and grandmother's funerals.

It hit me then that I even had to 'buy' salvation, or pay for my time in eternity. That was why the God that had appeared to Rev Neville seemed different.

Yet I was still not ready to commit to this Christian God, as I had had bad experiences with Christians in the past whom I felt were hypocrites.

During that period of searching for answers, I was also troubled by certain recurring dreams.

As a young girl of about 10 or 11 years old, I would dream of an eight-foot-tall pillar of light.

Puzzled as to what it meant, I asked my aunt, and she told me that

I could have met Jesus Christ in my dreams as He is known to be the "light of the world". I was sceptical and presumed my aunt's reply had to do with her being a Christian. So, I simply put the matter aside.

In early 1983, when the 36-year-old me was facing marital and work troubles and could not find any solution to my woes, I dreamt that I was in a boat surrounded by a sea filled with demons.

Distressed, I began to call out the name of an idol and it appeared. Even as the idol appeared on the seas, the same light that I saw in my childhood dream also materialised.

"Is Jesus calling me?" I wondered. In my heart, I knew Jesus was the light.

In mid-1983, I had another dream that I was enjoying myself at a party in my grandfather's two-acre bungalow at Upper Serangoon Road when a fire broke out. I, along with others, jumped into a boat at the river next to the house. I wanted to row the people to safety but, again, the sea of demons showed up.

I called out to the idol that I was familiar with and it appeared. Simultaneously, the filament of light that I had seen before in my previous dreams also came into sight and I woke up involuntarily singing a hymn that I had heard from my primary school days attending the weekly chapel at Fairfield Methodist Girls' School.

Shortly afterwards, while at a home meeting at Timothy's house, I heard a pastor from Ghana, Africa, preaching from John 15 about how unfruitful branches would be cut away and thrown into the fire.

I was afraid because I connected that to my three dreams and realised that, if I still resisted God despite His repeatedly calling out to me, that would be the outcome. I began to have the fear of the Lord.

Feeling convicted, my husband and I attended a service at Trinity Christian Centre that week. The preacher was Pastor Naomi Dowdy and she talked about man's folly in consulting astrologers and adhering to superstitions when it was God who created the stars and moon that astrologers get their readings from.

The friends who invited me to the church — Timothy and his wife, Connie — sat on the edge of their seats and kept turning to look out for my response, half anticipating that the bad-tempered me may stand up and shout at the pastor if I found the sermon message nonsensical. After all, I had done it before at one of their home meetings.

Little did they know that I was having my own personal encounter with God.

I felt that God was speaking directly to me, because the sermon message described all the occult activities I had been actively participating in. Then, I saw a vision of gold showers coming down on me and heard the sharp sound of metal chains loudly breaking within me. I felt as if a 100kg of weight had been lifted off me.

On 23 October 1983, in the home meeting of our other friends, CT Lim and his wife, Ai Hoon, who had also turned to Christ, I asked the leader all the remaining questions I had about the Christian faith. When he could answer all of them meaningfully, I decided to give my life over to the Lord that night in the home.

As I repented, the same filament of light that I had seen in my three dreams appeared and entered me. I felt the peace that the world could not give me. Suddenly, God and Jesus became so real to me. I pivoted with a 180-degree mindset change to dealing with problems no more my own way. I knew I was to follow Him and was also assured that I would spend eternity with Him.

During this time, my husband also had his own personal encounter with Jesus. So, from then onwards, my husband and I began to read the Bible and Christian books voraciously, and went from one Christian meeting to another, in our hunger and passion to know Him and His Word more.

When I shared this testimony of my exciting encounters with the Lord with Rev Norman Wong, my former pastor at Barker Road Methodist Church, he prophetically told me that "to whom much is given, much is expected". I kept his word in my heart, realising the divine calling in my life and my need to be obedient to God's leading.

Following these encounters, I also started to notice that I no longer experienced any migraines. When I told Dr Wong Yik Mun (my family doctor since 1975 to this day) that I no longer needed any medication, he laughed and said: "If all my patients are healed like you, I would have to close down my clinic!"

Subsequently, after I had several conversations about God with him, he shared with me that he had also started going to church.

Unlike the miraculous healing of my migraines, other changes for me did not happen overnight.

There was an episode at work when I continued to lash out at an officer in MAS with whom I was having a meeting.

At the time, magnetic ink character recognition (MICR) strips were being introduced on cheques in order to mechanise cheque clearing.

The smaller banks, which had only one machine to do so, needed some back-up machines for cheque clearing. I raised the matter but the MAS officer was not very forthcoming in rendering any support.

"If MAS won't do it (provide back-up machines), ABS will do it!" I said brusquely to the officer. I felt indignant because I knew ABS could do it and would do it if the authority would not intervene to help.

God later chastised me with His Word in Corinthians 4:7: "For who makes you different from anyone else? What do you have that you did not receive? And if you did receive it, why do you boast as though you did not?"

I was convicted and immediately put in my place.

Even though I was doing the right thing in seeking to solve a problem for the banks, I wasn't doing it gently. I was critical and arrogant. God showed me that, whatever capability or expertise I thought I had, it was not from me but from Him. I needed to extend to others the grace that I myself had received.

I later took the officer out for lunch to apologise to him, and MAS also eventually provided the back-up machines on their premises for the banks.

In a bid to rein in my temper and be quick to apologise when needed, I gave my staff permission to do a "stop" sign using hand gestures at any point during my discussions with them should they notice that I was getting carried away by emotion.

The sharing of my newfound faith also contributed in helping to train me for public speaking — a skill set I needed to master to take on media interviews on TV or radio whenever I represented ABS.

I used to freeze whenever the camera or recording was turned on and had to do multiple retakes.

Over time, many churches heard about my interesting testimony and invited me to share more over the pulpit.

As I began speaking more and more in churches, slowly, my nerves eased and I became more confident speaking in front of people and cameras.

This is not a book on Leadership or Management. Neither is it a book that intends to tout the accomplishments of ABS, of which there are many.

This book is Mrs Ong-Ang Ai Boon's personal sharing of her journey in life and how her personality and relationships were transformed. In her own words, she shares with us how she struggled in relationships, found purpose in life and fulfilment in family, friends, colleagues, and in Faith.

Though it was never intended to be, this book offers readers ample learning lessons in Leadership and Management, and on Relationships and Reconciliations. All will find comfort in reading this wonderful, first-person narration by the amazing Ai Boon, whose energy and sincerity always impress me.

Samuel Tsien
Former Group CEO, OCBC

Chapter 3

The Fleece Test

A year after I received Christ in 1983, and two years after I joined ABS, I found that my priorities in life had shifted dramatically.

Though I still found fulfilment and excitement in my work, I felt my family needed me more.

Once an alpha career woman decked out in elegant power suits, I was now prepared to lay it all down and become a housewife in order to spend more time with my husband and children.

My husband had yet to follow through with his ultimatum to leave me as he witnessed the change in me when I finally found the peace I was longing for. He also rededicated his life to Christ.

Despite my inclination to leave the organisation, however, I sensed that God wanted me to remain in ABS.

There was this resistance within me, as if the Holy Spirit was stopping me.

Like Gideon in the Bible who tested God's will by laying out a fleece, I decided to do the same to discern if staying in ABS was truly God's direction for my life.

At that time, ABS had a vacancy for an officer. So I told God that I wouldn't advertise for this open job position. If He wanted me to stay in ABS, He would show me a sign by sending someone to fill the position.

Thus, no job ad was put out and no one would have known that ABS was seeking an officer.

Within a week, I received a call from a close friend who asked me if I could offer a job to her nephew.

God had responded, but I was still hesitant. This young man only had an N-Level qualification, and I needed a person with at least tertiary qualifications.

So, I asked God for a second sign for further confirmation.

If this young man is the one You have sent, let him appear for the interview on Wednesday at 3 pm, without my arranging for it, I prayed.

Again, I received a call from the friend who had checked her nephew's schedule and asked if he could come on Wednesday at 3 pm.

Like Gideon, God answered both of the fleece tests that I had put out.

The young man was hired to be part of the team and he left after a year, while I did not resign from my job. Interestingly, the young man, his siblings and family members came to the Lord after his stint in ABS. I knew my time here was not yet up as I was convicted that God intended for me to remain in ABS.

First Faith Testing

With God now as my ultimate source of wisdom and guidance, I felt more anchored. No longer did I have to rely solely on my own effort and striving, which was exhausting and anxiety-inducing.

If I had assumed that life would henceforth be a walk in the park, however, such notions were quickly put to rest.

A year after both my husband and I came to the Lord, we experienced a major testing of our faith.

My husband had a dream in which the plane that he was on caught fire and he was told to bail out by jumping out of the plane.

Along with other details in the dream, he interpreted it as a divine instruction for him to leave his job.

That caused some degree of concern in the family as I would then be the sole breadwinner.

Despite our worries, my husband obeyed God and quit his job in 1984 to attend Tung Ling Bible School instead.

As a result, our family sold the extra cars, club memberships and scaled down on expenses for the children's tuition and food.

As one year passed, then two and then three without a second income, I went before God to ask: How long more, God?

He assured me that He would be with us and spoke to me about His perfect timing from a devotional passage in the book, *Every Day with Jesus*, by Selwyn Hughes. One of the lines in the book read: "I won't leave you in the oven a second too long or take you out a second too soon."

Shortly after, my husband and I began to clearly see the hand of God in providing for us.

My husband secured a job at Chemical Bank at the annual pay he asked for. The bank had refused to pay him that amount initially but came back to him to offer the same job on his stipulated terms a year later because they could not find anyone else. Later on, Chemical Bank's private banking division was acquired by Fortis Bank and he received yearly retention bonus pay-outs as a result.

Money also came in through different avenues; money which we did not know existed was suddenly returned to us. The income tax department refunded my husband $30,000 for the tax that they discovered he had overpaid over the years. Our real estate lawyer also reminded us that we still had a 10 per cent deposit, or $90,000, with him from a past real estate transaction that he would return to us, with interest.

We had either forgotten or were not aware about all these but God took care of our needs.

Monday and Thursday Fellowships

In those early years of faith, my husband and I were hungry to know more about God. We plunged into His Word and read it voraciously, and were often seen running from one faith meeting or conference to another.

On the morning of 1 May 1984, I was changed and all ready to go to a Full Gospel Business Men's healing conference held at the Meritus

Mandarin Hotel at Orchard Road.

On my way out of the house, I heard the still, small voice of God instructing me: "Do not go. Put into practice all that you have learnt."

The verse that came to me immediately was from 1 Corinthians 8:1, which says: "Knowledge puffs up, but love builds up."

Reluctantly, I changed out of my clothes and told my husband that God did not allow me to go for the conference. I had to stop hoarding head knowledge about Him, and start showing His love by loving others around me.

Later on, my husband called me from the conference and urged me to quickly make my way down as the preacher was baptising people in the Holy Spirit — a gift that I had been desiring.

No, I can't go down, I told him disappointedly but firmly, knowing that I had to obey God.

I felt affirmed by God for my obedience when I received a letter from a friend after the meeting. The friend said my presence was missed at the meeting and, as she was praying for me, the Lord directed her attention to two verses in the Bible.

The first was from 1 Corinthians 13:1: "If I speak in the tongues of men and of angels, but have not love, I am only a resounding gong or a clanging cymbal."

The second was from John 14:21: "Whoever has my commands and keeps them is the one who loves me. The one who loves me will be loved by my Father, and I too will love them and show myself to them."

The message for me was clear as day, and immediately applicable in my life. My obedience to His leading and Word was necessary.

As I grew in my relationship with God, what I talked about and was interested in inevitably began revolving around Him.

All day long, whether at work or elsewhere, I would talk non-stop about God. Colleagues and friends around me became tired about having to keep hearing about my latest 'obsession'.

"I will direct your talking," God told me, knowing that I needed an outlet to process my growing intimacy with Him.

He gave me the idea of starting a Thursday fellowship for the wives of my husband's friends. They were mostly housewives.

The irony was that prior to forming this group, I had few female friends. I found their conversation, or gossip, which centred around their husbands or shopping, insipid. I had long preferred the company of men, as they tended to talk more about world and current affairs.

Yet during this time, I was re-learning how to be a woman, and how to submit to my husband as a wife, according to God's ways. I found it helpful to share my struggles with other women and journey with them authentically.

In this way, I would have an outlet to talk and share about God, and a platform to reflect with other women on how we could apply our faith in the practical aspects of living. After all, God had instructed me to live out my faith, instead of accumulating head knowledge.

There was just one minor problem: The housewives could not gather to meet at night after my working hours because they needed to be home to cook dinner and spend time with their families.

So, I petitioned God with two conditions to be met before I went ahead with starting a fellowship group with these women. Firstly,

You need to help me clear my work calendar at 4pm every Thursday. Secondly, the women need to be able to commit to this day and timing.

Both conditions were fulfilled. The women committed their time to having the fellowship group meeting at my home, and I managed not to have any urgent or important work meeting at that time slot every Thursday since we started it in 1984. Over time, the Thursday Ladies Fellowship moved its time to meet later in the afternoon.

In the same year, I also started a Monday fellowship group for my office staff and workers in the vicinity to gather during lunchtime. Similar to the Thursday fellowship, I would share about what God had been doing in my life over the past week as I tried to put His Word into practice. The stories encouraged and empowered others in the group who had similar difficulties. I would have no-holds-barred conversations with them, about how I struggled with working with certain staff members under me and how God was training me to grow in gentleness and kindness.

The office workers, whether from ABS or offices in the neighbourhood, joined the group through word of mouth.

There was a time when a group of women from an American chemical company, Union Carbide, simply walked into a room in ABS to join the Monday group.

Their office was situated in the building just across ABS but they had not known of the lunchtime fellowship. They only found out about it one day when some of them stepped into a clothing shop at Plaza Singapura and heard worship music playing in the background.

As they made small talk with the shop owner, they casually asked her if she knew of any lunchtime fellowship group in the neighbourhood. The shop owner happened to attend my Thursday fellowship group and told them that I also had a group for office workers nearby at ABS on Mondays.

I never had to invite people to the group. It was by word of mouth and God sent people to us.

Having to helm the Monday and Thursday fellowships over the years — 39 years later, both are still ongoing — meant that I had to continually delve into the Word for wisdom. Such discipline ensured I immersed myself in the Word, keeping me afloat and refreshed to meet the challenges of life as they came.

Mini Revival

Even as a new believer, I was heartened to see that my faith influenced those with whom I worked.

In 1984, I met my Malaysian counterpart — the then Executive Director of The Association of Banks in Malaysia, Ms Chee Suan Lye — at the ASEAN Banking Council meeting in Manila.

I was being my usual self in being effusive about God in my conversations when Suan Lye turned to me suddenly and asked with disbelief: "You talk with God?"

I replied in the affirmative and shared with her how I came to faith.

When I returned to Singapore, Suan Lye would call me up every other day from Malaysia to ask me more about God. Unbeknownst to me, she was also searching for the meaning of life.

Later on, when she and her family came to Singapore, I took them to my church. In my church, Suan Lye accepted Christ and returned home to attend a church in Kuala Lumpur. Subsequently, she ended up marrying Pastor Paul Wong there. Today, they have four adult children and are active evangelists.

Even the people from public relations firm Form & Function, which ABS hired to do our annual reports, had life-changing experiences.

Whenever we had meetings together, I noticed that the firm's founder, Mr Ong Chin Ann, seemed somewhat guarded and distant. He would be slumped in his seat, with his arms firmly folded across his chest.

One Tuesday, I was about to leave my meeting with him to go for a lunch fellowship at St Andrew's Cathedral when I decided to ask him to come along.

He agreed, commenting that he used to go to that church in the past.

When he was there, he saw an old friend who was known for his promiscuous lifestyle and muttered under his breath: "Goodness, even this person can become a Christian!"

From then on, each time our project met with an issue, I would pray alongside him.

Once, our team was working on the collaterals for the ASEAN Banking Council as ABS was hosting it. During that crucial period, my deputy Lucy Kwok slipped and twisted her ankle. Chin Ann remarked in despair: "Oh dear, you won't be able to work tomorrow." Being the organisers of the event, we had a heavy work schedule ahead and her absence would set us back.

Immediately, I jumped in and prayed for healing for Lucy, who is also one of my prayer warriors.

The next day, Chin Ann could not believe his eyes when he saw Lucy walking normally, with barely a limp.

Then, we also had to print a brochure for the conference at the last minute because the data came in late.

"Look, even if I can print, the colour separation cannot be rushed as the colour won't dry. It won't be ready in time," Chin Ann told me. Together with Lucy and my secretary Linda Phay, we prayed in earnest for the brochure to be printed on time.

The next day, Chin Ann came to me and said with a laugh: "I don't understand. It's a miracle. The colour separation was amazingly trouble-free and it dried so quickly."

He would later join me in my Monday lunchtime fellowship, and he rededicated his life to Christ there.

"All my life I met people who would only take and take from me, and I was the one giving and giving," he told me. "But when I met you, I realised that because you are so giving, I became the receiving one."

His associate Anu Suppiah, who had also backslid in her faith, commented to me during a ride in the car one day: "I have never worked with anyone who prayed in the office like all of you do — it's faith in action." There and then in the car, I led her in a repentance prayer and she also went back to the previous church that she used to attend. She met her husband-to-be there and is a happy grandmother today. Both Chin Ann and Anu are still good friends of mine now.

On the home front, my mother, having witnessed the dramatic change in me, also received Christ the following year in 1984. She immediately shared the Gospel with her mother, then 84 years old and living in Kuala Lumpur. Grandma became a Christian in 1985.

My grandmother moved to Singapore to live with us after her conversion and was fervent in her walk with Christ, reading the Bible daily. On the eve of her returning home to the Lord when she was 89 years old, I visited her and she said to me in Teochew: "Boon, thank you for introducing Jesus to me. I am going to heaven and the streets are paved in gold. I will go first and wait for all of you there. In the meantime, you continue to diligently obey and serve the Lord."

She went home in her sleep that night with peace and a smile.

A Furnace that Refines

From my dramatic entry to ABS to my wanting to resign barely two years later, from my husband issuing me an ultimatum of his intention to walk out of our marriage to my coming to Christ, the early 80s were my crucible years that made me dig deep to find the answers to questions I was seeking: Who am I and what is my purpose? Who am I as a leader?

Slowly, I realised that the key lies not in what a leader does, but who a leader is, especially in the face of trials and tribulations.

ABS is my furnace. It breaks me and reveals who I am. Daily, as I die to self, amid continual work and life challenges, I become a bit better at leading and loving others.

This once 'sleepy hollow' would come to play an invigorating role in the financial sector. As ABS grew in trust and stature with key players in the industry, it also moved from its old office at PIL Building along downtown Cecil Street to the MAS Building at the invitation of the central bank in July 1985 — an address that money can't buy.

But there would be many tests for me and this fledgling Association in the years to come.

Chapter 4

Near-Death Experience

In 1985, I almost died.

At that time, China was opening up and I was scheduled to accompany the then ABS Chairman, Mr Allan Ng (former Deputy Chairman of UOB), on a trip there. He was leading a delegation of 25 representatives from local and foreign banks to foster ties with the Chinese.

Interestingly, two months before the trip, I felt I needed to tell my deputy Lucy Kwok to get her passport ready.

Naturally, she asked why. I didn't know and couldn't explain it either, but I simply repeated my instructions to her to just get her travel documents in order.

Of all times, my wisdom tooth had to act up just a week before the trip. I knew I'd better get it fixed before I travelled, so I headed to the dentist. He extracted the tooth and prescribed me some antibiotics.

I am all settled then, I thought. But who would have foreseen that I would break out in hives over the next two days?

One evening, I suddenly felt faint while removing my makeup in the bathroom. Immediately, I went to lie down on the bed and asked my older son, Tze Lin, who was in the room to call his father.

I found myself fast losing consciousness, and my breath getting colder and colder.

Yet, I was still aware of my husband telling the three children and his mother to get down on their knees to pray for me.

As I listened to him praying to the Lord for me to get well, I realised I was also slipping out of my body through my head.

An Unusual Vantage Point from Above

I felt myself floating away and I could see from the ceiling in the room a formation of the five of them kneeling by my bedside praying for me as my physical body remained still and straight on the bed.

I couldn't help thinking to myself then: "What a lovely prayer for healing and of them telling the Lord how much I am still needed and loved… A prayer worth dying for."

I stopped floating when I reached the corner of the bedroom. I couldn't move further and was stuck up there for a while. Suddenly, I felt myself descending and my breath getting warmer and warmer. What exactly was happening to me?

I realised that I was re-entering my body again through my head from where I had left. As I fit back into my physical body, it felt just right — just as how a hand fits perfectly into a glove.

Then, I heard Tze Lin say: "Look, Mum is pink again."

Apparently, my face had been ashen grey throughout the ordeal, and they had thought it was the remaining smudges of colour from my eye makeup and mascara.

The next morning, my husband called my office and told Lucy what happened. "Ai Boon will not be able to go on the China trip."

Lucy, who then had to go in my place, felt both surprised and amazed. She recalled that I had prophetically prepared her in advance to get her passport ready.

She added: "You should have called me as my cousin is a doctor and he could have made his way there to help you."

"If I had waited for the doctor instead of praying, Ai Boon would have been brain dead," my husband replied.

Dr Wong Yik Mun, my family doctor, diagnosed me with anaphylaxis. He explained that I was being suffocated; I was not able to breathe as my airways had been blocked from the swelling arising from my allergic reaction to the sulphur in the antibiotics I had taken.

Dr Wong then administered another medication (an antihistamine) to me. It sent me hyperventilating.

In the end, he could not do anything but advised me to flush out the sulphur from my body naturally by drinking copious amounts of water.

The effects of the allergy were bad. My body was swollen from the top of my head to the soles of my feet. The itch was terrible and I was in constant pain.

In the middle of the night, I was listening to the gospel singer Jimmy Swaggart singing when one line from the lyrics — "Stand up and be healed in the name of Jesus ..." — caught my attention. Desperate for some relief from my condition, I spontaneously responded to the 'command' in the song by jumping out of my bed and standing by it. As I did that, the same tall shaft of light — which I had seen in my previous three dreams and which also came into me the night I received Christ in 1983 — entered me.

Immediately, I was completely relieved of the pain and itchiness. I was miraculously healed, though my body was still swollen. A couple of days later, the swelling subsided and I was back to my normal self.

After this experience, God became more and more real to me. I learnt how to depend on Him so that I would not be easily troubled whenever I met with problems in life.

After all, not many people survive such surreal out-of-body experiences.

In my walk with the Lord, there were many other incidents of a supernatural nature which were foundational in building up my faith, in understanding the power of the Word and in increasing my dependency on the Lord. I know that even as I face challenges in the office or at home, there is an almighty God and His Word that I can rely on.

My close shave with death also gave me a renewed ability to roll with the punches and adapt to unforeseen circumstances as they came.

For instance, China was not the only communist country ABS visited. In May 1989, ABS also organised a trip to the USSR, just before the Berlin Wall fell. The eight-member delegation visited various banks and government agencies in the USSR.

The then ABS Chairman, Mr Wong Nang Jang (EVP, OCBC), and I remember the trip well, but it was not because of the Russian leaders we met.

We were on a train from Moscow to St Petersburg. When we arrived at the railway station, Nang Jang and I were informed that we had to share a cabin.

It turned out that the rest had paired up among themselves, according to the same gender, and there was only him and me left to occupy the last cabin.

That began the big story that night, the next day and the whole trip after that — that Nang Jang and I had spent a night together in one cabin in an overnight train.

Though we became the butt of the jokes, it seemed the only practical thing to do since there were two separate bunk beds in each cabin. I had learnt not to be squeamish and to go with the flow. Anyhow, Nang Yang is an old friend who had headed Citibank during the years when my husband was working there.

The Terror in the Office

When it came to work matters, I was not only pragmatic, but also perfectionistic.

I set high standards for myself, and therefore I also held certain expectations of my staff.

Whenever they could not do what I thought was relatively

manageable, or whenever they did not see things the way I did, I could not understand or empathise with them. Anger and frustration would overtake me quickly.

Once, my accountant, Ms Ng Soo Moi, could not explain an issue satisfactorily to me. I felt so exasperated when I could not understand what she was trying to tell me that I began talking in a raised voice.

Shortly after she left my room, my secretary told me that the accountant had gone to the toilet to cry after our tense conversation. I realised I had gone over the top with my intense emotions and had unintentionally upset her. Immediately, I went to the toilet to look for her to apologise and explain myself.

I told Soo Moi that I wasn't upset with her but was actually frustrated at my own inability to understand her explanation. I realised then that I needed to have the spiritual fruit of self-control and gentleness when dealing with others.

What helped me was venting these emotions to my diary and going to the Lord with them. It helped me to deny my fleshly self on subsequent occasions.

Over time, my accountant began to understand me better and did not take me too seriously whenever I expressed myself unbecomingly.

Knowing how I am and realising that I am a 'work-in-progress' in the Lord, I would urge my staff to pick up from me only what was useful. Just like how they eat fish — eat the flesh and throw away the bones — I hoped that they would learn from my strengths but ignore my temper.

On another occasion, I apparently spoke so loudly and harshly to a bank representative in a consumer banking committee meeting that Mr

Peter Heng, then a representative from UOB, called me on the phone straight after the meeting.

"Do you realise that your behaviour (towards the woman) at the meeting just now was unbecoming? You are a bully," Peter told me honestly.

I appreciated his frank comment as I knew he was not being unfairly critical. I didn't realise that I had inadvertently been arrogant and callous.

Feeling bad that I was not as gentle or kind as I wanted to be, I immediately picked up the phone and called her. I told her about the feedback that I had received from Peter and apologised. She appreciated my call and accepted my apology graciously. We became good friends and worked well together after that.

From this incident, I learnt to be more conscious of my remarks and behaviour at subsequent meetings and encounters.

My struggle with reining in my temper and tongue was not only confined to my peers and subordinates.

There was once I complained to former UOB economist Mr Tan Joo San about my differences in opinion with my bosses. I strongly disagreed with some of the decisions they had been making.

Joo San looked at me calmly, and reminded me that I am a Christian. He pointed me to Romans 13, which called for believers to submit themselves to the governing authorities as those were instituted by God.

His reference to the Scriptures shook me as I had not realised that His Word has also prescribed obedience to authority, and that this mattered to God.

When I went back to read the Romans passage, the words "therefore he who resists authority has opposed the ordinance of God; and they who have opposed will receive condemnation upon themselves …" convicted me so much that I felt I had been shot between my eyes.

I felt convicted of my argumentative posture and the strong stand that I took on any issue. I repented and agreed to obey His Word.

This was a pivotal occasion that led to a change in my attitude. I became humbler and more respectful towards authority figures, and was able to be more courteous in my dealings with them.

In my earlier days before I received Christ, my notorious reputation for being difficult to work with often preceded me. When I was in MAS, HR would laugh at me, telling me that no one liked to be transferred to my unit. Then upon joining ABS, I recall a particular council meeting when one of the bankers who had just walked in casually asked the then ABS Chairman how the Association was doing.

"It's fine, except for the uncontrollable Director," came his frank reply. Everyone knew he was referring to me. I had also overheard the remark.

I wasn't upset as I was aware that he was speaking the truth.

Prior to me being convicted by the verses in Romans 13, I just accepted such descriptions of myself with resignation. This nature of mine seemed unchangeable. I had strong views and tended to be domineering unless I was convinced otherwise. It was just me and not many people could take it. I could not change myself even though I really wanted to, not until I had the empowerment of the Holy Spirit and the Word to do it.

Good Luck and Good Riddance

On another occasion, when it was time for the ABS Chairmanship to be rotated from OUB to OCBC, the outgoing Chairman and then alternate Chairman of OUB Mr Peter Seah said matter-of-factly to the incoming Chairman Mr Wong Nang Jang and myself: "Good luck to you, Nang Jang, and good riddance to you, Ai Boon."

Again, I was not offended by his comment. Peter was a long-time friend whom I had known since our campus days in the University of Singapore. I knew what he said was a statement of fact and I was determined to work on myself to make a change.

"Just you wait, Peter, by the time you are back as Chairman, I will be so transformed that we will become friends," I vowed silently.

That was because the ABS Chairmanship is rotated among representatives from the local banks every two years, and thus the Chairmanship was due to be rotated back to OUB, or potentially Peter, in six years' time. True to my word, when he was rotated back to be the ABS Chairman once again, we had many good conversations together and enjoyed a pleasant working relationship.

I often got myself into various conflicts with others because I suffered no fools. The irony was that God had also once called me a fool.

It happened when I was ranting to Him one day after having an argument with one of my sisters. When I quietened down, He directed my attention to Proverbs 18:2: "Fools have no interest in understanding; they only want to air their own opinions."

Slowly, I began to see the ugly parts of myself and I did not want any of it to remain.

To be an Oak Tree, Not *Tau Gay*

I hated the fact that when I was under the anointing, such as when I shared at the Monday and Thursday fellowships, I could be very calm, like an angel with self-control.

But when I headed back to the office and something got me riled up, I could become like a devil and not be as gentle and kind as I expected myself to be by then. I was so disillusioned with myself and my behaviour, that I lost patience with God's work in me, because of the seemingly protracted period of my transformation.

Discouraged by my lack of progress, I challenged God. I told Him that if He didn't change me, I wouldn't talk about Him anymore. What was the point? I didn't want to be a hypocrite.

He responded gently and said: "I want an oak tree in you, not *tau gay* (beansprout)." An oak tree takes a long time to grow, has the strength and hardiness to withstand the storms of life and offers protective shade to those who seek shelter under it. But a *tau gay* sprouts overnight and has no deep roots or character.

He gave me Isaiah 61:3: "They will be called oaks of righteousness, a planting of the Lord for the display of his splendour."

I realised that God's work in me might take some time — or actually, a lifetime. I needed to be patient with His process of transforming my character so that I would have the deep and extensive root system of an oak tree. The Lord was not looking for an outward behavioural modification, but rather an inner transformation.

Time was a crucial ingredient to the work-in-progress within myself, but it would not be the crux of my transformation.

Instead, a life-changing revelation for me came from a prophetic word given by a speaker at one of my Thursday fellowship sessions.

The Lord, through the speaker, revealed to me that the cutting and harsh words that came out of my mouth were an inevitable outflowing of a "faint" heart and a "sick" head. Isaiah 1:5–6 describes how the unhealed and untreated wounds of a body can cause revolt and rebellion:

> "Why should you be stricken again?
> You will revolt more and more.
> The whole head is sick,
> and the whole heart faints.
> From the sole of the foot even to the head,
> there is no soundness in it,
> but wounds and bruises and putrefying sores;
> they have not been closed or bound up,
> or soothed with ointment."

I was astonished. I didn't see myself like this, but God did. I thought I was always the bad one hurting other people. I didn't realise I was hurting inside.

I was causing hurt to others because I myself am sick and in need of healing.

Part 2

Growth Through Struggles

Chapter 5

Projecting Rejection

Over the years, I have gradually come to realise how profoundly my mother's rejection of me had affected me.

Growing up, my demeanour was the exact opposite of my mother, a soft-spoken Teochew woman. She was gentle, sweet and full of self-control, while I was loud, domineering and had a hot temper like my father.

"If only you were more like me and not like your father" was her constant refrain to me.

We often did not see eye to eye, and quarrelsome clashes between us were common.

Even after I was married and had my own family, my bickering with my mother persisted. She continued to nag me, saying: "You already have three children but your behaviour still hasn't changed one bit."

Such comments — regularly dished out — may have been well-intentioned by those from the older generation, but they left me feeling deeply rejected and misunderstood.

Similarly, whenever my friends failed to see my point of view, I felt that they did not seek to understand me and I saw them as rejecting me.

Rejection and Projection

At work, it was clear to others that I did not like to be contradicted; I was seen to be unreceptive to new ideas and suggestions. That is, until the day I had an epiphany.

My eyes were opened to the fact that the root of all this behaviour could likely be my mother's rejection of me, and that my attitude towards the staff in the office was a result of my projecting her rejection of me into those situations.

After having such a key revelation, I began to do the necessary inner work to find healing and freedom.

One strategy helped me tremendously.

Whenever I began to react to any opposition to my suggestions, I would quietly, in my own mind, forgive my mother for not understanding me. That helped me become more open to other viewpoints and not take their rejection as a rejection of myself as a person.

I realised I was also shaped by my familial environment in other ways, including my love for dressing up.

My mother was the quintessential Teochew wife — beautiful and demure. One of my younger sisters was so pretty that everyone around her dubbed her Lin Dai, a gorgeous and famous Hong Kong actress from the 1950s.

By comparison, I felt I was not much of a head-turner. However, I noticed that whenever I wore a new dress, people would compliment me. That not only motivated my desire to dress up, it also became an obsession. I would buy new clothes every week, and always ensured that all my accessories were well matched with my attire. If I wore a nice dress for an occasion, it would be rare for me to wear it again. I would not be caught dead wearing the same dress if that particular group of people had seen it before.

In the banking industry, there are many women who dress stylishly in a way that makes them look both feminine and professional. We do need to dress well according to norms and occasions. However, there were times when I overdid it out of my own insecurities and a need for acceptance.

The Naked Dream

One sign that there was more to my need to dress up came via a vivid dream that I had in the mid-1980s.

In my dream, I was walking along North Bridge Road and Chinatown (where I grew up) with two senior ABS officers, my deputy Lucy Kwok and Diane Chai. As we turned into Upper Cross Street, I noticed that the corner shop was a textile retailer. The shop displayed bales of cloth next to a long, standing mirror.

When I looked into the mirror, I saw, to my horror, that I was naked. Immediately, I reached out for a bale of cloth and covered myself with it. I then turned to the two ABS officers in indignation and asked why they had not alerted me to my nakedness. They did not reply me; one of them looked as if she had an answer but was holding her tongue.

When I related the dream to my husband, he alluded to my fierce nature by replying: "They would not dare to tell you the truth."

I saw the dream as God's way of showing me the nakedness that I felt as I navigated life with feelings of guilt and shame of being 'not enough' — not good enough, not pretty enough and not smart enough. As a result of low self-esteem and a lack of self-acceptance, I had been trying to clothe my nakedness with worldly cloth in seeking approval and attention through power dressing, and exerting a strong and dominating personality.

The dream was my version of the story of Adam and Eve who used fig leaves to cover themselves up after they disobeyed God and found themselves naked. As God covered them with animal skins, I would later discover — when I became a Christian — that He has also given me the robe of a slain Saviour whose blood covers me.

In the meantime, I saw myself like a crab, with a seemingly loud and confident armour as its exterior, but with a soft interior. Inwardly, I was quite diffident and emotionally fragile.

Ms Cindy Yim, an officer in MAS who once reported to me and is now a good friend, used to explain to others what I was like by saying: "Ai Boon is okay when you really get to know her. Don't be afraid of her."

I also used to tell my staff that my bark is worse than my bite. "At least you know where I am coming from as I would tell you things as they are, and not do you in from behind."

Nonetheless, these should not be a vindication of my brusque behaviour.

As I went to God with this new level of awareness about myself, He gave me Isaiah 61:10, which spoke to me about God clothing me in a "robe of His righteousness".

Only God can provide such a robe. I can't cover myself up with my effort or ability. I can't work for it or buy it. I can only receive it by faith and through grace.

In 1998, I visited Israel for the first time with a group from my church. We visited a diamond factory and were enraptured by the stones. My husband saw me looking at a 1.3 carat solitaire and told me he would buy it for me if I really liked it. As I contemplated this and was about to say "yes", the Lord asked me: "Would this diamond cover your nakedness?" I did not buy it in the end. I learnt to focus less on earthly things and more on the things of God.

Thus, in spite of my vanity, I tried to put God first. When I was a new Christian, I asked the Lord if I needed to be less vain or be more modest in my dressing. He simply replied: "You can remain vain, but put Me first." I understood it to mean to seek Him and He would provide for all my needs. Practically, that also meant not stressing over the need to have new clothes or to coordinate my outfits with the correct accessories.

The first test in this area would come shortly after.

You Look Lovely Tonight

One morning, as I walked into office, I was greeted by my secretary Linda who remarked in horror: "Mrs Ong, you have a cocktail tonight!"

I immediately knew what she meant. Linda was asking why I was not dressed as formally and stylishly as I would normally be if I were going to a function straight after work.

I had forgotten about the work cocktail and my instinctive reaction was to go home and change.

In the split second when I was contemplating whether to head home, I heard God saying: "Put Me first." I knew I had to obey His instruction and go as I was. So, I relaxed and continued with work until it was time to set off for the cocktail.

I was received at the event by one of the hosts, the former Managing Director of MAS, Mr Michael Wong Pakshong. Despite my simple dressing, the usually stoic Wong — who does not dispense compliments easily — said to me: "You look lovely tonight."

It seemed like God was winking at me through this curious episode. I was elated, not so much because of the compliment but by the fact that God had been true to His Word.

It was a confirmation of the truth in His advice for me to put Him first and trust Him, instead of relying on my dressing. Perhaps there was a radiance about me when I learnt to relax, and I began to understand why my husband would say "beauty is skin deep" whenever I asked him for comments on how I looked in a particular outfit. My aspiration later shifted from outward adornment to the hidden person of the heart instead, who in being quiet, gentle and reverent, is precious in the sight of God (1 Peter 3:3–4).

To be Loved is to be Known and Understood

Due to the rejections I had received over the years, I realised I harboured a hardened heart — one that was unable to receive love, whether from God or people.

Yet as I reached out to God, He began healing my heart.

There was once when I had yet another heated argument with my mother, who by then had become a believer.

I was opposing her views by quoting Scripture and my mum retorted back in anger: "If a Christian acts like that, I don't want to be a Christian."

However, God later spoke to my mother during her quiet time to help her understand why I acted the way I did. He gave her Isaiah 66:2, and my mother realised that God "look(s) on with favour" at me because I "tremble at (His) word".

When my mother told me how God explained my behaviour to her, I felt vindicated.

To me, to be loved is to be understood. I felt loved when God not only understood me, but also when He helped my mother to understand me.

My mother had received Christ a year after I became a Christian. We used to visit mediums together but she came to the faith after witnessing the change in me. When she became a believer, she also changed radically. Instead of lamenting to me the usual refrain of "Why can't you be more like me?", she instead asked God: "Lord, I want to be like my daughter." She had seen me spending much time with God and she wanted to have the same degree of intimacy with Him.

Another time when I felt seen and known by God was when I was facing a major issue at work which could have potentially blown up very badly. I was so stressed by it that I was not only unable to eat my dinner, the chopsticks I was holding were shaking vigorously from the trembling of my hand.

I left the dinner table for my bedroom and went on my knees to pray about the matter. Lo and behold, when I opened my Bible, it flipped open to Isaiah 44:8, which says: "Do not tremble, do not be afraid … You are my witnesses. Is there any God besides me?"

There I was trembling at dinner, and then I read a line that exhorts one not to tremble nor be afraid. I felt known, understood and loved by God. That's how He softened and healed my heart bit by bit.

As I learnt how to receive love, giving and expressing love to others became much easier.

When my younger son, Tze Ru, was about eight years old, I was showering him when he innocently narrated to me the order of his affection towards everyone at home. His top favourite was his father, followed by Grandma, then Grandpa, his older brother and sister, our dog Royal and then, lastly, myself.

I knew he was just stating facts and I simply took it as a challenge to raise my position on his 'totem pole'. I knew I had succeeded partially when the boy matured into a teenager and professed that when he has his own house, he would want me to live with him. Who would have known then that his wish would come to pass eventually, though not according to our plan, when I moved in with his family later on under very different circumstances.

The World Spins Faster with Globalisation

While I was busy dealing with my inner demons that affected my leadership, the pace at work was also intensifying.

As Singapore recovered from the 1985 recession, it was also entering into new territories in the 1990s, especially in the financial sector. Former Managing Director of the MAS, Mr J Y Pillay, in a prescient speech given at the ABS' Annual General Meeting in 1987, outlined three key trends.

One, financial markets were going to go global. Two, there would be increased volatility in financial markets. Three, there would also be the rise of securitisation, a process of financial engineering that repackaged risks and assets to raise funds and capital.

These trends would significantly impact banks. In order to thrive in such a fast-paced environment, banks needed to groom their talent, grow their expertise and branch into new areas of banking.

In this brave new world of finance, the close working relationship between MAS and ABS was a key strength in helping banks navigate the new normal. "It is to the advantage of banks that they discuss their problems, as well as their aspirations and plans, with the Authority on a confidential basis. Close rapport is not confined to a select group of banks," Pillay said. .

The 1990s saw the growth of both the breadth and depth of Singapore's financial activities. Capital markets, debt securitisation, bonds and syndicated loans were already part of the landscape. These were complex activities that boosted Singapore's standing.

ABS was keen to help firmly establish Singapore as a proper international financial centre. Apart from working with MAS on regulations, ABS became an active member in policy consultations. The Association had to step up in its role to help grow Singapore's standing as a financial centre.

Chapter 6

I Will Teach You

In the early 90s, Mr Lim Ho Kee, Chairman and CEO, UBS East Asia, brought in an Egyptian academic, Dr Moneim el-Meligi, who was known for his management programmes, to train C-suite leaders in both the public and private sector.

I was keen to attend to learn more about effective management strategies and approached the HR department of DBS, then the Chairman bank of ABS, for its support. I received its approval and was about to submit my application form for the programme when I heard the Holy Spirit say: "You don't need to attend this. I will teach you."

So, I obeyed and did not apply for the programme.

In the following years, God showed me which aspects to focus on for my job — it was not knowledge of management, but building trustworthiness among members and stakeholders in the industry. Expertise can always be tapped on through the banks but trustworthiness had to be learnt by myself with His Word and leading.

The Potter Moulding the Clay

God started teaching me by first moulding my character through small occurrences in life.

Once, on my bedroom floor, I was peering over a two-page spread in the newspaper and reading about the success of a local beauty chain. I found out how the founder, who used to be a secretary, was on holiday in Europe when she chanced upon a slimming franchise and brought it into Singapore to immense success.

"How can a secretary amass this amount of financial success while here I am, having a university degree, yet earning a small monthly salary?" I griped to God.

I heard a voice within me say: "You cannot serve two masters; you either serve Me or Mammon."

"I will serve You, Lord!" I replied spontaneously.

God would later show me that walking the talk is no walk in the park, and how the love of money is also linked to the spirit of envy and greed.

The true condition of my heart was exposed in an incident when a friend called me to share how she had won an airline ticket to London from a lucky draw with just a supermarket purchase.

I became envious and asked the Lord why others were so lucky. Instantly, I received a rebuke that went: "What good is an air ticket for you when you can't even travel by air?"

I used to have an inner ear imbalance that caused me severe nausea whenever I travelled by air. Even being on a fast-travelling lift could make me feel sick. Thus, whenever I could, I would avoid travelling by air.

God's rebuke set me free. I saw that it was so easy to be envious, even when it may not be to my benefit.

If I continued to carry such a spirit of envy to the workplace, that would mean that the organisation would be competitive instead of gracious and generous. Others would not find ABS to be a trustworthy partner.

Instead, ABS fostered a collaborative and open culture by organising seminars and other training sessions to share information freely and readily with other relevant partners rather than hoard industry knowledge or expertise by limiting them to its own members.

Another aspect of my heart that God dealt with during my working days was of me harbouring a critical and judgmental spirit.

There was a time when I attended a management presentation conducted by a well-dressed and articulate woman who had a strong personality. While listening to her, I felt that she seemed arrogant and domineering.

On another occasion, a gentle and soft-spoken man conducted a similar session and I thought well of him.

Who would have known that I would later meet both of them at a party in a friend's home and find out that they were actually husband and wife! I laughed in my heart, wondering how such a gentle man could live with such a domineering woman.

At that moment, God spoke to me from Matthew 7:1–2: "Judge not, that you be not judged. For with the judgment you pronounce you will be judged, and with the measure you use it will be measured to you."

Then, my eyes were opened and I saw the likeness of myself and my husband mirrored in the other wife and husband pair that I was silently mocking.

I realised that I was also an alpha female who had a gentle giant as a husband. I saw the ugliness in myself for judging others, and repented.

Through the years, God also used how I treated "the least" in my household to mould me.

I once had a domestic worker who was particularly clumsy and slow when doing the housework. She would drip coffee all over the floor when carrying the cups out; the food she cooked was also substandard.

One day, the helper made an extremely silly mistake and I raced down the stairs, ready to unleash the full force of my displeasure upon her.

But when I was running down the stairs, I heard a voice saying to me: "Whatever you did for one of the least of these brothers and sisters of mine, you did for me." I stopped in my tracks as I was immediately chastened.

Knowing that my helper loved chicken wings, I learnt to show love to her by offering her chicken wings before giving them to my children. When my helper eventually became a believer, I also taught her to pray before she cooked.

There was another time when I discovered that another helper was moonlighting, and I immediately intended to send her home. But God reminded me: "Let any one of you who is without sin be the first to throw a stone at her" (John 8:7).

So instead of sending her home, I decided to counsel her.

I realised that such acts of daily dying to self was the path God wanted me to take, instead of simply getting head knowledge by attending meetings or conferences. These incidents humbled me and reminded me that God is no respecter of persons.

Fear and Favour

Apart from working on my character and values, God also showed me that He is the one true authority. Whenever situations get difficult or murky, I am to seek the favour and have the fear of the Lord, not of man.

There was a time when I feared the disapproval of a senior officer from MAS.

I can't remember exactly what I did but I had made an error. The style of this senior officer was to call up both the boss and the underling who made the mistake and he would hold the boss responsible for it. So, when my ABS Chairman and I were summoned to see him, I was very afraid.

In the middle of the night before the next day's meeting, I got up to pray. I noticed that on my husband's Bible was a card with the verse Isaiah 41:10–11, which says: "So do not fear, for I am with you; do not be dismayed, for I am your God ... those who oppose you will be as nothing and perish."

I believed the verses were an assurance from God and was greatly comforted. The next morning, my husband told me that he had been praying for me and he had received those verses from God for me.

That morning, I also prayed with Linda, my secretary, before stepping into the meeting room with my Chairman.

The situation that greeted me when I went in was the opposite of what I had expected. The senior officer received us warmly, and asked if I needed further support for the project that I was handling. Even the assistants of the senior officer looked puzzled as everyone had expected me to receive a shelling.

What this taught me was to look to God, and that helped me to lay aside the fear of man. There was so much fear in me, but the Word of God came and encouraged me.

During that period of time in the late 1980s, I also had some friction with people from a government agency which I had to work with quite frequently.

Sometimes, in our jobs, we may inadvertently do certain things that result in others rejecting us. So, I must have done something that offended them and they were giving me the cold shoulder. The disfavour was something I could not afford to have as the nature of my job meant that I needed good relationships and open doors to get advice or have informal consultations.

Troubled over the matter, I sought God. He gave me the verses in Isaiah 8:12–13:

"Do not call conspiracy
everything this people calls a conspiracy;
do not fear what they fear,
and do not dread it.

The Lord Almighty is the one you are to regard as holy,
He is the one you are to fear,
He is the one you are to dread."

God told me to just leave it up to Him, and not to fear them. That set me free.

The next time I met them, I just spoke to them confidently, as if nothing had happened between us. Amazingly, everything indeed went on henceforth as per normal.

There are times when I meet work challenges that could cost me my job. But I have learnt not to fear the rejection or disfavour of man, which may be unpredictable, and not to depend on my own power and ability as well, because I am also vulnerable to making mistakes.

My confidence comes from depending on God and His Word to guide me.

Shoring up Foundations before Entering a Heady, Golden Era

The moulding of my character and values, guided by a reverential fear of God, would give me a firmer foundation to lead ABS into the heady first half of the 1990s — a golden period of growth for Singapore and the financial sector.

Economic growth averaged nearly eight per cent a year, boosting standards of living. Singaporeans would start to talk about the five Cs: credit cards, condominiums, cars, country club memberships and cash. The sun was out and there seemed to be nothing that could stop Singapore as it roared ahead.

Chapter 7

Covering the Naked

In the late 80s, a senior official from the MAS commissioned ABS to produce a publication on the topic of "Singapore: An International Financial Centre".

The plan was for its Managing Director to present it to his international counterparts in a meeting that he would be attending in Basel, Switzerland, in five months' time.

I sought out and engaged the advertising agency Batey Ads, an established firm that had created the iconic Singapore Girl for Singapore Airlines. The company assigned a service manager to work with me on the project and I gave him the brief for the publication.

The first draft of the publication came with a cover picture of a seated gypsy woman gazing into a crystal ball — symbolism for her looking into Singapore's future. I promptly rejected the illustration.

He was visibly taken aback by my objection to it and asked why. I told him that I am a Christian and consulting soothsayers was unacceptable. He understood and replaced it.

During the course of working together on the project, I noticed that he was often slow and lethargic in picking up calls, responding to revisions and meeting deadlines.

I was very frustrated with him for lagging behind in the work because I had to provide regular progress reports on the book to the senior MAS officer. Yet I also realised that I had told him I am a Christian, so that restrained me and I knew I had to 'behave myself' in managing him.

Taking the Blame

I could only complain bitterly to the Lord by journaling all of it down in my prayer diary daily. As I sought the Lord, he spoke to me through Isaiah 58:7 "...When you see the naked, to clothe them, and not to turn away from your own flesh and blood?"

I understood God's instruction on the matter: I cannot reveal or criticise his shortcomings publicly as it would shame and discredit him as if he were "naked", but instead I ought to cover and protect him from being found out.

It was a painful process and a tall order from God because whenever I met the MAS senior official to give an update on the progress of the work, I had to come up with excuses, such as the delay being due to my inexperience and oversight, thus taking the blame.

While God knew I would obey as instructed in reverence to Him, He also knew it would be a really difficult experience for me. Thus,

He motivated me to persevere with His instructions by giving me His promises that followed in Isaiah 58:8–9: "Then your light will break forth like the dawn, and your healing will quickly appear; then your righteousness will go before you, and the glory of the Lord will be your rear guard. Then you will call, and the Lord will answer; you will cry for help, and He will say: Here am I."

These promises were precious to me. They would come to pass in subsequent years in my times of need, especially when my husband became critically ill and had to undergo a heart surgery.

Nevertheless, this assignment was very trying and my old self still wanted to see vindication and justice. I was in much despair and cried a lot. Whenever I had to go for the meetings where I received the ire of the senior MAS officer, my deputy Lucy comforted me.

I thought of how Jesus must have felt taking on the sins of the world when he was completely innocent. Here I was, only asked to 'carry' the sin of one person and it was so painful.

Halfway through the project, the senior MAS officer came to the realisation that the service manager was not pulling his weight and was stalling the project. He instructed me to take the project off him.

I dutifully made an appointment with the manager, went to his office and waited for him in the Batey Ads boardroom. Suddenly, I heard a loud audible voice declaring a simple statement: "His soul is more important than ABS."

Startled and in a state of awe of the voice, I did not dare take the project from him. When he arrived, I continued discussing matters of the publication with him and left.

I was in a daze that whole afternoon. I had obeyed God, but I was also troubled as I did not do as instructed by the senior MAS officer.

Fearful and anxious at my disobedience to the official, I called one of his assistants to relate to him what had happened, and asked him what he would have done if he had been in my shoes.

The assistant replied: "What boss tells us to do, we do."

That comment left me feeling insecure, and I wondered whether I was being too emotional as a woman and questioned my own management capability.

I felt foolish. As I thought about my foolishness, I remembered the verse that says: "The foolishness of God is wiser than human wisdom." I went to my Bible to look it up.

As I flipped the pages of my Bible, another verse from the next chapter in 1 Corinthians 2:5 jumped out at me, as if God were speaking directly to me that my "faith might not rest on human wisdom, but on God's power". God wanted me to trust Him.

Those verses comforted me tremendously and removed my fear. I became surprisingly calm and had the confidence to face the senior MAS officer the next morning to tell him that I did not take the project from the manager as he had instructed. When I related what had happened at the Batey Ads boardroom, he listened and simply said: "I will hold you responsible for the publication to be completed in time."

When I walked out of his office room, I looked up to God and said: "I am calling on Your letter of credit" for the publication. I had obeyed Him and trusted that God Himself would be responsible for the project, not I.

As I continued to work on the publication with the manager, he persisted in his recalcitrant ways.

One day, during one of the meetings, he remarked to me: "You are one of the nicest clients I have ever worked with."

I could not help but blurt out: "Well, I had to complain to God and write to Him about you in my diary, that's why you don't get it from me."

A Private Revealing

He was surprised and asked if he could read my diary. Immediately, I said: "No, it's between me and God!" I knew all the nasty things I had said about him to God in the diary and it was private. But he reasoned with me that "it may be good" for him to do so. I then told him that I would pray about it.

I later agreed to let him read my diary and he invited me to lunch, reminding me on the day itself to bring my diary along.

At the lunch, I instructed him to read only the parts in the diary that had his name in it. Those were the portions where I would rant to God about him, complete with expletives, as I had been really upset with him.

I had written all of it down and sent it all to God — and to the Cross. As I poured out all my strong and intense emotions to Him, it was a release and I felt unburdened after doing so. It had allowed me to remain cool and collected when dealing with the manager.

As he read the diary, I could see the expression on his face change and I felt embarrassed at all the nasty things I had written about him and his work.

When he finished reading the journal entries, he said to me: "You have a unique relationship with God. Thank you for not taking the project away from me. I truly see the grace of God in this."

I was surprised and he continued speaking: "I am a Christian from the Church of England but have backslidden and not been back to church for a long time. When I return home, I will return to church."

I learnt that he was leaving the company and returning to the United Kingdom, and would be handing the project over to another colleague. I told him that when the publication was out, I would send him the first copy. I eventually did.

However, in the meantime, the publication still had some way to go in order to be completed on time. A new designer was appointed to work on the book and it was submitted to the printer when it was done. An elderly Chinese man from the printing company cautioned that they might not have enough time to have it typeset, colour separated and printed. I told him in simple Mandarin to simply do his best and we would trust in God for the rest. He smiled and said: "Since you put it that way, okay."

Though the responsibility to complete the job on time was taken off him, the elderly Chinese man worked on the printing job through the weekends and was even late for his family dinner during the Mid-Autumn Festival. Grateful for his commitment, I gifted him with two boxes of mooncakes.

In the end, the publication was printed in such a timely manner that it was delivered to MAS just a few hours before its Managing Director was due to fly to Basel later that day. I was well pleased with the outcome of the project and its blessed ending. I then asked God how I should tell others about this testimony. He quoted from Jeremiah 1:12: "Tell them that I watch over My Word to perform them."

From this episode, something broke in me. I have learnt to obey and fear God rather than Man as God is faithful when He speaks. I began to depend more on the leading of the Lord, and learnt that I need not be too quick to protect, explain or vindicate myself in self-defence, especially if it could be of help to someone else's well-being.

For instance, if an issue with an employee or work partner were to crop up, I would go directly to the person to talk and offer guidance instead of exposing the weaknesses or errors of my subordinates or bosses, unless it is an illegal act.

I was serving as the Executive Director of the Consumer Association of Singapore, CASE, for one-and-a-half decades. In my role I had many interactions with Ai Boon who represents the banking community.

I recollect the many confrontations and challenges we had with one another over various financial industry matters. Both of us in our work capacity were doing our utmost to fiercely represent and protect the interests of our respective stakeholders. Some interesting disputes we both worked through together included disputes ranging from hard selling of Structured Deposits to susceptible and vulnerable consumers; to consumers complaining of unauthorised Credit Card transactions; to questionable bank charges on consumer spending overseas; and to mortgage loan interest changes during the tenure of the loan.

I used to wonder where and how this marvellous lady found her energy and strength to deal with so many matters under her charge and yet was able to engage the stakeholders in CASE. Whenever we met, she would say, "Seng Choon, officially we can disagree and fight over disputing matters, but personally we can still remain as friends." That made me wonder even more — was she was my 'opponent' or my 'friend'?

In the early 2000s, it was Ai Boon's tenacious spirit that led to the setting up of a Consumer Dispute Unit in ABS. Later in 2004 together with MAS and various stakeholders an industry-wide dispute resolution mechanism, FIDREC was formed as well as a series of national financial educational programmes put together for consumers.

If I could describe Ai Boon, it would be her Zest for Life!

She would attend to every matter with a deep sense of determination, responsibility and commitment. She would always ensure an amicable solution was found.

I am humbled by her goodness, kindness and grace. In fact, I have learned much from her rather than she from me.

I cannot help but mention this, though. At the end of each conflict resolution and settlement, Ai Boon would come out with a beaming smile. Seeing her trademark smile, I knew that she had already entrusted the whole matter to her God.

Seah Seng Choon JP, PBM
Former Executive Director and Adviser, CASE

Chapter 8

Submitting to Authority

I had passed the test of protecting those who worked for me, but I would still have some way to go in learning to submit to people who were placed above me.

In the early 90s, I was unhappy with a government department for being difficult over a particular matter. So when my then ABS Chairman Mr Ernest Wong (former President of UOB) told me to draft a letter to reply to the department, and to start it with the line "I am pleased to advise ...", I refused.

I preferred to address them with less sentiment, and instead go with "In reference to the matter ..."

Though I did not want to comply with his instructions, Ernest insisted on it. He told me to draft it his way and to bring the letter to him for his signature. He then asked me to see him after work that day.

Immediately, I knew that I was in trouble with my boss. Throughout the rest of the day, I felt bad about my behaviour and repented for my disobedience.

When I went into Ernest's office, he began the conversation with: "Ai Boon, I hear you are a Christian now..." He was alluding to my insubordination and stubbornness, which was jarring in light of the Biblical value placed on submission to authority.

I confirmed what he had heard and shared with him that I had received Christ when I was desperately seeking to change myself, especially when my husband had wanted to walk out of our marriage. I admitted that I was very bad-tempered, strong-willed and domineering, and that God was still doing a work in me.

With such candour, a good conversation followed. We ended the meeting with my request to him to give me feedback on my conduct as I let the Lord further work on me. He agreed.

A few years later, Ernest and I both found ourselves in Thailand as we needed to attend an ASEAN Banking Council meeting. While we were on our way in a bus to Pattaya where the meeting was held, he turned to me and said: "Ai Boon, you had asked me to give you feedback on yourself. I must say you have indeed changed, but there's still much more improvement needed."

I was not discouraged but was, instead, inspired by his comment. Even as I sought to "die to self" daily, I knew I was still a work-in-progress and needed to press onward to the call of God in my life.

My target was to be more like Jesus in character and to develop the nine traits of the fruit of the Spirit: love, joy, peace, patience, kindness, generosity, faithfulness, gentleness and self-control. I was better than before but far from the target.

Even my younger son Tze Ru, who was eight years old then, could tell me to my face: "Mum, your fruit has worms!" I also agreed and prayed to God for Him to please cover whatever small fruit that was growing with newspaper to stop the fruit flies from laying eggs and producing worms in it.

Along the way, I have also learnt to submit to authority even when my superiors have different faith convictions from me.

I remember an occasion when there was a visiting speaker to whom we needed to present a token of appreciation. As it was the year of the dragon in the Chinese zodiac calendar, I was asked by the then ABS Chairman, Mr Wong Nang Jang, to buy a gold-plated dragon figurine as a gift for the speaker. I hesitated to do so given my Christian conviction.

However, I was under the authority of the Chairman, and knew that obeying God's Word and my inner conscience meant that I needed to submit to all authorities. Thus, I did as I was told and purchased the figurine.

Interestingly, on the day of the presentation, I was pleasantly surprised to hear Nang Jang telling me: "I know you are a Christian. Therefore, I will present the figurine to the speaker instead." Instead of my having to do so, he took over the task and explained the significance of the dragon in the Chinese zodiac to the speaker.

Submission to Husband

When I first became a believer, I also struggled with submitting to my husband, as commanded of wives in 1 Peter 3:1, whenever we had disagreements.

I told God that I could not submit to him because I felt I was still in the right when we argued.

God's response was simple.

"Will you submit to Me?" He asked.

"Yes," I replied.

"Then you submit to My Word. What does My Word say?"

I answered: "To submit to my husband."

"Then you submit to My Word, despite how you think or feel. Obey My Word."

With that, I resolved in my heart to obey God's Word, and therefore to submit to my husband. It was a transaction of the will, not of sentiment; the first step I took to restore my marriage.

It was not easy for me but I had made a commitment to God. In my moments of anger after having a disagreement with my husband, I would release my intense emotions to God by hitting the pillows on the bed or wringing water out of the towel if I was in the shower. I also raged and complained in my journal by sending all the emotions that were weighing on me to the Cross.

During a particularly intense conversational prayer session, I remember that I got so angry with God that I even took a wet towel and threw it in the air at Him. I didn't find that strange because God is absolutely real to me when I talk to Him. I also know that I don't need to worry as He is God and He can definitely take my candid expressions.

In having these outlets of release, I would then not need to take my anger out on the people around me. I found myself calmer and better able to submit after venting my emotions in those ways.

A Videotape Playback of Regrets

When my late husband Hock Chye had a heart attack in 1996, I pleaded with God to spare his life to give me more time to be a submissive and supportive wife, and to redeem the years when I had been such a difficult wife for him to live with.

It was on a Saturday afternoon, while having lunch, when my husband suddenly felt his chest tighten. Beads of perspiration furiously rolled down his forehead.

Recognising that these may be symptoms of a heart attack, I asked him if he would like to be admitted to the hospital.

No, he replied.

Was he prepared to die at home then, I probed further.

He said "yes".

So for that weekend, both of us chose to linger in the presence of God instead of fretting over his health. We prayed, worshipped and read His Word.

As usual, I returned to the office on Monday. In the early afternoon, my husband called and told me that he was ready to be admitted to the hospital.

When I met him at the hospital, the cardiologist informed us that the heart attack had only occurred that very afternoon on Monday.

To me, I felt that the Lord had given us a warning ahead of time for us to be anchored in faith and in the Word before Hock Chye underwent an open-heart surgery for three blocked arteries.

Throughout our time in the hospital prior to his surgery, I kept hearing the cardiologist mumbling under his breath that they were "going to lose this chap".

However, my heart was not troubled. Instead, the chorus of a song kept looping itself in my head: "On Christ the solid rock I stand, all other ground is sinking sand, all other ground is sinking sand."

Thus, I had the peace of God. My husband eventually managed to pull through.

However, he could not return home yet as some complications had set in after the open heart surgery.

One night, I was at home when I received a call from the hospital alerting me that my husband was "in distress".

When I arrived at the hospital, I saw the doctors applying the defibrillator on him.

Immediately, I went out of his room, fell to my knees and spoke to the Lord.

I asked the Lord not to take him home as I would die from having regrets, as His Word in 2 Corinthians 7:9–10 describes. I asked Him to give me an opportunity to repent and be a good wife to him as he had all along been the long-suffering husband. I felt I still had not done enough for him.

At that moment, I began to see a vision of a videotape playing before my very eyes. It traced the times when I had been a difficult wife to my husband — often argumentative, demanding and unreasonable.

Immediately, I repented and sought the Lord's mercy. In response, God gave me the verse from 2 Chronicles 7:14, which I appropriated for my husband: "If my people, who are called by my name, will humble themselves and pray and seek my face and turn from their wicked ways, then I will hear from heaven, and I will forgive their sin and will heal (Hock Chye)."

With the assurance that my husband would be well, I set my heart to repent from my "wicked ways". To me, it meant bearing the fruit of the Spirit and obeying His Word in my behaviour. I also realised the need for me to seek the Lord and depend on Him more rather than relying on my own opinion and taking matters into my own hands.

God made good on His promise to me. I had called on Him and, according to His promise to me when I covered the nakedness of the service manager from Batey Ads, the Lord indeed came through for me. After three months of going in and out of hospital after his initial surgery, my husband was finally discharged.

The cardiologist was amazed by his progress and remarked to him: "It's a miracle you are alive." Then he turned to me and said: "You are a woman of great faith." I responded: "No, I don't have great faith but a great God."

I would not know the full extent of my prayers on my husband until one evening, many months later, when we attended a fellowship gathering at a friend's home.

The visiting speaker for that evening was Pastor Henry Hinn from Regent College, brother of the well-known televangelist Benny Hinn.

As Hinn delivered his message that night, he suddenly stopped and turned his attention to my husband.

"Brother, I do not know you but you have a valve in your heart that cannot close. The Lord will heal it," he said.

My husband and I were taken by surprise as that medical condition was only known to the both of us and the cardiologist who had advised my husband to return to have the valve fixed.

On his next visit to the cardiologist, the valve was indeed successfully closed.

At that meeting, Hinn also gave us a glimpse of what went on behind the scenes when my husband was fighting for his life in the hospital. Hinn said to him: "Brother, you are alive today because of your wife's prayers."

The prophetic words from a stranger who had no prior knowledge about our circumstances encouraged our hearts and built up our faith. It was an external confirmation that the Lord had indeed heard and answered my prayer that night, else things could have turned out very differently.

My husband would go on to live for another 10 years, till he succumbed to a severe infection due to complications from dialysis in 2006. His kidneys had started failing two years before that. During that time, I remembered my promise to God and submitted to my husband by taking good care of him.

I submitted to His Word to be kind and gentle. My vision was to develop into the hidden person of the heart, with a quiet and reverential spirit that is precious in the eyes of the Lord (1 Peter 3:4).

When my husband died, I remember my niece, Valerie, commenting to me: "Aunty Boon, seeing the way you were looking after Uncle Hock Chye, I expected him to live to a hundred."

The Second Resignation

Loving my husband by submitting to him granted me a second lease on life with him. I would also find that submitting to my bosses somehow led me to also have a second lease on life at work as well.

In 1994, I found myself too overwhelmed with work and contemplated quitting. This was during UOB's Chairmanship of ABS by Mr Ernest Wong.

During this stressful period, I sought the Lord in His Word and He told me in 2 Chronicles 20:17 that I "need not fight this battle ... stand and see the salvation of the Lord on your behalf ... do not fear or be dismayed; tomorrow go out (to face your boss) for the Lord is with you."

Not knowing what to expect but having received the Lord's instruction, I made an appointment to meet my boss the next morning to discuss a "personal matter".

When I met him in his office at 8.30am, I broke down and wept as I related to him the stress I had been facing from all the projects that were on my plate. I told him that I was considering resigning from ABS.

He remained calm despite my distraught and emotional state.

He looked through the list of projects that I was handling, smiled and told me to come back after freshening myself up.

When I returned to the meeting room 15 minutes later, he had all the relevant executives seated at the table.

He said to them: "Ai Boon needs some help with the ABS projects. Please work with her." He promptly delegated the projects to each of them.

I felt so relieved and it seemed as if a ton of weight had been lifted off my shoulders.

His parting words to me that day — "everything can be resolved" — was a life-lesson. It has helped me face my vulnerable moments and taught me to handle my staff in the same manner as he had done for me. I learnt to better understand the needs of my subordinates who might not be able to cope with juggling several projects.

From him, I saw that submitting to authority may involve humility and correction, but it also comes with the protection and guidance I needed for my growth. These were lessons of leadership that I internalised as I began to come into my own as a leader.

As I grappled with relating to difficult subordinates, and learnt how to submit and obey to the authorities placed above me, both at home and at work, a national cleaning up was also underway.

A National Cleaning Up

ABS needed to step up its role at the national level to keep the banks in line, since Singapore's status as a financial centre needed good governance and codes of conduct to raise the standard of its services.

Back in the 70s and 80s, for instance, gambling was almost a customary tradition among forex traders in the banks. Forex trading is relentless — markets do not stop for lunch. Yet as and when they were able to sneak a break, traders would huddle in a corner to grab a game of three-card poker or blackjack.

As the 90s rolled in, improper behaviour like gambling was not the only issue plaguing Singapore's banks. They were also bedevilled by poor practices on the service front. High and unfair bank charges, frequent failures to notify customers of such charges and even unauthorised trading were prevalent. Banks were also high-pressure selling credit cards along Orchard Road by setting up makeshift sales counters.

These activities resulted in a rise in complaints to MAS. As customers' dissatisfaction rose, public trust took a hit. This erosion in confidence was something that Singapore could ill afford as the city-state looked to establish itself as a regional financial powerhouse.

Reputation of the banking industry is sacrosanct. Singapore aimed to be the Switzerland of the East — we had to be squeaky clean. How could you have your traders gambling on the floor?

While the MAS had successfully established a solid compliance framework that led to exponential growth in the financial sector, it was not completely foolproof. Moral loopholes still existed that could be exploited.

ABS, on the behest of MAS, moved swiftly to address the cracks before they became chasms. To prevent MAS from intervening with disciplinary action, we took the initiative to formulate a plan to keep the banks in line.

Behind closed doors, a committee at the Association was in the process of drafting a code of conduct that aimed to ensure that the industry was at a standard that was sterling.

The document would be the first of its kind for Singapore's financial sector. Such a code would foster a higher level of professionalism and enhance our standard as a sound financial centre.

ABS released the long-awaited code in 1993. The elaborate 30-page booklet spanned more than 120 clauses, split into three sections: A general code of conduct for all bank staff; sound procedures for banks engaged in the security business and proper practices for the conduct of treasury activities.

Over the years, the code of conduct has played an unsung, but formative, role in establishing the solid levels of trust and repute that Singapore's banks hold globally today.

Trust grew as the rogue behaviour whittled away. With the code as a guide, banks worked to solidify customer confidence. Such was its effectiveness that drafting codes became ABS' approach of choice whenever the need for new standards arose.

Over the years, the Association piled on further guidelines to maintain the code's relevance. From the original three in 1993, they have since more than doubled to seven, covering areas such as corporate finance, asset management, securities/brokerage and treasury/fixed income business.

As the banking landscape evolved, ABS also churned out more codes to help banks better improve their increasingly multi-faceted operations, whether it was a code of advertising for banks, a code of practice for credit cards and unsecured credit, or guidelines for handling customers who lacked mental capacity.

Over the years the continuous efforts of ABS, in partnership with the regulator MAS, to establish good banking behaviour have paid off. Singapore is now home to a well-oiled financial industry that effectively runs through self-governance — a crucial factor that has bolstered the Republic's standing as a leading financial hub.

Part 3

Turning Point

Chapter 9

I Hate You, Mum

I was alone in my hotel room one night during a work trip to Sydney in the early 2000s when I began to be aware of an intense longing in my heart.

"Mum, I miss you, I need you," I blurted out into the empty, still air before me.

There was no one there to hear these statements, honest and raw, but the act of speaking it out and hearing myself say it unlocked something within me.

I was then a middle-aged woman in my 50s, and it was the first time I was calling out for my mother, wanting her love.

By then, I knew I harboured some resentment towards her for all those years of feeling misunderstood and rejected by her.

But I did not know the depth of my longing for her love, nor realised how much I loved her.

There is but a thin line between love and hate, as I would find out later.

When I first became a Christian in 1983, I was convicted to submit to God's Word to honour my father and mother.

By then, my father had already died. We had a good relationship because I took after him; we both wore our hearts on our sleeves, liked to take charge of things and had a hot temper.

My mother was the opposite of us; she was a beautiful, gentle and submissive Teochew woman who often chastised me for my loudness and brashness. "If only you could be more like me, instead of your father," she would bemoan.

Growing up, I also hated the fact that she favoured my two brothers over my sisters and me. The boys received most of her attention and they would get special food and attention that were not given to us.

Whenever I expressed strong opinions that she did not agree with, we would get into unpleasant clashes.

I felt misunderstood and rejected by her, not only because we had vastly different personalities and ways of seeing things. Even when we quarrelled, I hated the way she would not stand up to me and speak up.

Instead, she was scared of me. The diffident way she talked to me even when she disagreed with me irritated me further.

It felt like another form of rejection.

Whenever people at the office shrank back in fear and talked to me with much trepidation in response to my loud and strong persona, I felt the same form of rejection.

So it seemed easier to love my mother from afar.

Keeping Mum at Arm's Length

She used to live with my younger brother and his family. At times, I would try to fulfil my filial duty by inviting her to stay with me for a short while.

Inevitably, we would end up not seeing eye to eye and clashing with each other. By the time the week was up, I would send her packing after yet another heated argument.

Yet whenever Mum returned to my brother's place, a fruit basket would follow her shortly after.

It was my way of apologising to her and was an aspirational act on my part to remind myself of my desire to bear the fruit of the Spirit in my life.

Several hasty departures and fruit baskets later, Mum finally understood what I was trying to do.

"I know that if I leave, a fruit basket will come to me," she would joke cheekily to me later on.

Despite these efforts, things between us remained fraught. Deep within myself, there were still unhealed wounds of resentment because I did not feel fully understood and accepted by her.

When my mother battled colon cancer in 1992, I could not even bring myself to visit her after her operation in the hospital.

Being in the same space as her was too stressful and distressing for me. I did not want to be at loggerheads with her during a time when she was vulnerable and recovering.

So, I prayed about this issue that was troubling me and I came down with a bad cold shortly after.

Thank God! Now, I had a legitimate excuse to not visit my mother face to face in the hospital. I was actually grateful for my timely illness.

Asking after her on the phone was sufficiently distant enough for us to not trigger each other, I figured.

So I continued living with this strange tension within me — having a desire to honour my mum yet being unable to fully embrace her due to deep-seated emotional baggage lodged within my soul.

"I Hate You, Mum!"

When I returned to Singapore after the work trip in Sydney, the hectic pace of life resumed and I shoved the newfound realisation of how much I longed for my Mum to the recesses of my mind.

One day, I was on the phone with Mum when we got into yet another one of our disagreements.

In the midst of it, I suddenly, and emphatically, said: "I hate you, Mum!"

Over the phone, I heard her shocked reply in English: "Oh my gosh."

I cannot remember how we continued the conversation after that, but I knew something significant had happened.

When I finally articulated those repressed feelings, which were subsequently received and acknowledged by my mother, I felt such a release. Years of suppressed resentment left me when I could directly express them to the person who had caused those hurts.

For too long, it had been locked up within me. To say such a thing to my mother, an elder whom I loved and respected, was unthinkable.

Yet when it finally came out in the open, I was relieved.

Then, I thought of Richard Gere having a chat with Julia Roberts on a balcony in my favourite movie, *Pretty Woman*. He was recounting to her how he had been spending time on his psychologist's couch and paying a million dollars for therapy to learn how to say "I hate you, Dad" to his father. "That set me free," Gere told Roberts.

Similarly, I was set free, and I laughed silently at the thought that, fortunately, mine was achieved free of charge.

From that moment onwards, I was set free in the sense that I could freely forgive and love my mother.

I noticed the change within me when I would find myself giving in to her demands, even if they seemed unreasonable. This was made possible because, when I relinquished the grudges I had towards her, I suddenly found that I had the capacity to understand her better.

Conversations between us could continue without being punctuated with fights or disagreements.

The most convincing sign — that a breakthrough had indeed happened — was when I offered to take my mother in to live with me in 2009 after my husband died in 2006.

I even moved out of my own double-storey apartment to rent a single-storey apartment without stairs so that it would be more elder-friendly for her.

Mum, too, changed the way she related to me. Her constant refrain of "if only you could be more like me" eventually evolved to "God, I want to be more like her", especially during the moments when she witnessed how close I was with God.

Mum would live with me for the next 10 years until she died peacefully in her sleep in 2019.

Grace Upon Grace

I recognise God's grace in my reconciliation with Mum. In the long journey of overcoming my feelings of anger and bitterness, as well as in my ability to finally accept Mum for who she was, it was His grace that made it possible.

Being a recipient of His grace enabled me to extend the same grace to my daughter whenever relations between us became rocky. When she was young, she used to be terrified of me. As a result, our relationship was strained during her growing up years.

As a young adult, she once became so angry at me that she threw a clothes hanger directly at me. The hanger missed its target, and I picked up the hanger as if nothing had happened.

Just as I had experienced a deep emotional release from surfacing my hidden emotion to my mother, I also gave my daughter the grace she needed to be 'set free', even if it came in the form of a flying hanger.

Today, we enjoy a close relationship, even though she is living with her family in Melbourne, Australia.

Chapter 10

Turning from Red to Black

About one or two years before my reconciliation with Mum, ABS also experienced a major turning point of sorts.

It all started with my church's service which was then held every Sunday at the Grand Copthorne Hotel. We had a guest speaker, Ian Yaxley, from New Zealand that Sunday morning.

As he was walking past my seat to head to the pulpit to deliver his sermon, he suddenly turned around and said to me: "The Lord is going to transform your business from red to black."

Business? What red? What black? I didn't really understand what he was talking about because I did not run any business then.

What he said surprised me, but I did not give much thought to it.

During that period of time, I happened to be mulling over the issue of how I could serve the smaller foreign banks better. We were supporting the services and interests of the local and larger foreign banks quite well and I wanted to do more for the other smaller foreign banks in the industry.

So, I enlisted the help of Mr Ronnie Teo, a former senior bank executive, to accompany me on my visits to 30 banks from different countries.

When we met them, we asked: What are your needs? What can ABS do for you?

This was around the time when Singapore's financial sector was opening up to the rest of the world as she rode the wave of globalisation. In 1999, MAS introduced a five-year programme to liberalise access to Singapore's domestic banking market.

At that time, MAS was also issuing many consultation papers on policy developments as it wanted to evaluate the policies' impact on the industry.

In response, the smaller banks told us that they needed help from industry experts to analyse these consultation papers in order to gauge the impact on their businesses, and to assess if there were any concerns regarding these policies that they needed to give feedback on.

They suggested to me that ABS could hold industry-wide briefings by engaging consultants and lawyers with the relevant expertise to give their take on these policy developments. They would then not need to engage their own consultants which would be costly. With such economies of scale, the whole industry would benefit.

The smaller banks would also be keen to go for such briefings as they would be able to hear from the bigger banks on how they would be handling these banking developments.

In 2001, ABS started organising these briefings at hotels, charging a small cost-plus fee for attendance. This was the first time the non-profit organisation started generating income for itself.

In the past, it used to survive from hand to mouth by relying on funds generated from its annual membership fees. However, by every November, ABS would run out of funds and would have to ask the 18 bank members on its Council to pay the next year's membership fees in advance to tide it over the next three months before the rest of its members would pay their fees in January. When the following November arrived, the same tight financial situation would reoccur.

A Council member had even called ABS an "insolvent association" during a year-end budget meeting.

Things started looking up, financially, for ABS from 2001.

Apart from gaining income from organising briefings for the industry, unexpected funds would also come in from another novel outlet.

Credit Bureau Singapore

At that time, banks were beginning to aggressively embark on a large-scale issuance of their own credit cards and introducing other unsecured retail credit products. Thus, the banks needed to ascertain the credit risks or indebtedness of customers before granting them credit facilities. MAS also saw the need for this, especially since this was in the aftermath of the Asian Financial Crisis.

ABS began to look for a vendor to set up a credit bureau for such a purpose.

It was then that I recalled an American commercial data and analytics firm, Dun & Bradstreet, paying me a visit in the past to offer its credit bureau services.

"Don't call me, I will call you," I had told them then, as the banking industry had no need for such services at the time.

So, I thought of them when we were searching for a vendor and called them up, not knowing that they only offered corporate credit information services, not consumer credit. Therefore, they would need to find a partner before venturing into this project. At that time, they were in a confidential merger discussion with a local partner, Infocredit. Infocredit was then in a separate discussion with Baycorp, the main credit bureau operator and debt collection agency from New Zealand, and together, they jointly bid for the project, alongside three other major companies.

The three major companies found the Singapore market too small and did not offer any proposals.

Thus, Inforcredit, Dun & Bradstreet and Baycorp, together with ABS and an ABS committee that comprised 10 representatives from the banks, began working on the project. From the data provided by the banks that had credit card facilities, they came up with a database that could consider a customer's credit risks, not by the net worth of the person, but by their loan repayment histories with the banks.

It was not an easy task. Consensus had to be reached on what form of data to provide, how to define and analyse the data, as well as what type of products to develop. We had to make sure that the data submitted by the banks and financial institutions were understood and interpreted in the same way by everyone and that the assessments of the customers' credit risk were done transparently.

It was hard for everyone to be on the same page as there were many banks and committee members involved. It was such a tall order, akin to herding cats (known for their independent behaviour). During a meeting when the discussion was going nowhere due to numerous dissenting opinions, I jokingly remarked: "I thank God that He so loved the world that He sent His only begotten Son to save the world, and did not depend on a committee, or else Ai Boon would still not be saved."

We worked on this project for two-and-a-half years with the service providers, which burned much money in the process. However, we had yet to get the regulatory approval from MAS to launch it, as MAS was diligently going through their proposed operations and controls with a fine-tooth comb. This was a necessity given that this company would be holding all the retail banks' customers' data. The existing terms in the Banking Act also did not make provision for a credit bureau, so Credit Bureau Singapore had to be later recognised through an amendment in the Banking Act.

With no apparent light at the end of the tunnel, Baycorp told me one day that they wanted to be dropped from this project if I was still unable to give them a timeline as to when the project would receive the necessary approvals. It had been taking up too much of their time and money, yet there was still no guarantee that it would be given the green light.

I told them: "I can't tell you when, but you cannot drop off the project!" Surprised, they asked: "Why not?" I bluntly replied: "Because

I like you!"

They stayed on and shortly after, MAS gave its approval.

As the inking of the contract between the consortium and ABS was finalised, and the project was tabled at the ABS Council for endorsement, the Council gave me an unexpected piece of advice. They reminded me that it is not ABS' core business to run a credit bureau. Rather, they urged me to let the professionals run and operate it, while ABS could maintain control of its management policies by being on its Board. With this change, the contract, which was slated to give the consortium 25 per cent and ABS 75 per cent of the shareholding, was now reversed. ABS would instead hold 25 per cent but have control of the Board.

As it turned out, this change was very important. The additional shares of revenue meant that the Credit Bureau has been able to refresh its technology regularly, enhance its product offerings and maintain the service level to its members.

Credit Bureau Singapore (CBS) was recognised by the *Government Gazette* on 23 August 2002 and it started operations that year. The launch was timely. MAS now permitted customers to have credit cards with a three-month salary limit.

By making information available to assess a borrower's repayment history and ascertain their creditworthiness, CBS helped financial institutions not only reduce their risk of loan defaults and delinquency rates, but also grow their business at the same time.

The success of CBS could be attributed to several unexpected factors. At that time, prior to the enactment of the anti-competition law in

Singapore, ABS was able to include in its bye-laws a requirement for all its member banks with retail customers to be a member of CBS. This ensured that the data in the bureau was comprehensive as it was an important ingredient for an effective credit bureau. The bye-laws were later amended when the new anti-competition law came along.

CBS also became a useful tool for the banks as MAS had expected them to make credit enquiries on new applications and review checks on its customers' repayment history on a regular basis. Employers in the public and private sectors also began to request for their potential employees to give their consent to obtain their credit bureau reports for employment screening and other checks.

As a result of the growing demand for credit bureau services, CBS turned operationally profitable after 18 months and distributed dividends soon thereafter. ABS thus began to have another income stream — yearly dividends from CBS. It started with some $200,000 a year from 2008, and now it contributes at least $1.5 million annually into ABS reserves. On its 20th anniversary in 2022, CBS also declared a special dividend of $2 million for ABS.

The Association would also generate a third income stream later on.

In 2012, the London Interbank Offered Rate (LIBOR) scandal came to light. LIBOR is a global benchmark for interest rates on everything from credit cards to trillions of dollars in financial derivatives. Bankers at several major financial institutions were found to have been colluding with each other to manipulate the rate.

Following the LIBOR debacle in 2012, it became evident to MAS that the rates had to be administered by an entity that it licenses and regulates.

Thus, ABS set up a fully-owned subsidiary, ABS Benchmarks Administration Co (ABS Co), specifically to own and administer ABS Benchmarks in Singapore: Singapore Interbank Offered Rate (SIBOR), Swap Offer Rate (SOR), the Singdollar Spot FX and the Thai Baht Spot FX. All these rates were calculated by the then Thomson Reuters, now known as Refinitiv. Hitherto, the rates provided by ABS for the industry had also been calculated by Reuters since 1998.

As a company, ABS Co needed funds to run its full suite of corporate functions. Therefore, users of SIBOR and SOR rates, which had previously been provided gratis, would now have to pay a fee. Although the fees charged are not high, they enable the company to generate some profits each year.

From 2017, ABS started receiving yearly dividends from ABS Co, which amounted to $1.3 million that year.

From Deficit to Surplus

In the early 2000s, when I noticed that ABS was starting to be able to bring in its own funds, I realised that the prophecy of the guest speaker from my church that Sunday morning was accurate and was slowly coming to pass.

I may not have a business of my own, but I was running ABS and, indeed, our coffers had been in the red. In 2007, we had a deficit of over $600,000.

With funds coming in from these three income streams, our finances were finally in the black in 2011. By the end of 2022, ABS had a retained surplus of over $11 million.

Such surpluses came in handy to benefit the industry. The Association's total annual membership fees had not been sufficient to cover its increasing yearly expenses, given inflation and other factors. However, with these additional funds, we have not needed to raise membership fees over the last two decades.

ABS has also been utilising the surpluses to defray costs whenever it organises seminars, conferences and courses for its members. It also uses the surpluses to fund industry projects and other networking and training sessions.

It has been exciting to see the prophecy come to fulfilment. It built up my faith and dependency on God, knowing that He is our ultimate provider. I saw His fingerprints and guiding hand throughout these developments of the day.

All these enabled ABS to become a unique association that found creative ways to serve its members and the industry without raising membership fees much.

Numbers Are Not My Forte

Though I have been in the banking scene all my life, and I lead an organisation in an industry that deals with billions and trillions of dollars, I am not good with numbers.

Some people find that funny, but it is no joke.

Even in university as an economics major, I avoided taking papers on statistics and accounting. I took two history papers instead and graduated with a degree in Social Science.

Whenever I go out for lunch and have to foot the bill, my eyes glaze over the receipt. Sometimes, the figures 'dance and float' before me and I am unable to make sense of them.

Once, my accountant, Soo Moi, saw me buying something and fumbling with the change, and she remarked: "Mrs Ong, if I didn't see this with my own eyes, I wouldn't have believed that you really cannot handle numbers."

Such a weakness of mine did not matter much as I was not a banker, but I ensured that I understood the relevant ABS accounts and budget. I also played to my strengths instead, such as having the gift of hospitality in organising and hosting events, the ability to come up with solutions to intractable problems, and the people skills to rally and unite parties with different interests.

Questions of Financial Misappropriation

Yet there were times when challenges arose in this area of my weakness.

In 2000, the ABS Council was looking through the budget when a member raised a red flag. He pointed out that about $100,000 was raised through a project but it was not reflected in the accounts.

Where was the money?

I could not answer or explain away the query; neither could my accountant, who was equally baffled.

As we were unable to account for the money, the then ABS Chairman

Ernest Wong had no choice but to send in the internal auditors from his bank, UOB, to check the books.

"Mrs Ong, I did not take a cent," Soo Moi, my accountant, desperately pleaded with me.

I believe you, I told her, but there was nothing I could do to alleviate the seriousness of the situation we were facing.

Well-meaning Council members called me up to ask if I was all right, as the possibility of fraud or malfeasance was hanging in the air.

On the morning of the day when the auditors were due to come in, I gathered the staff team to pray together in the meeting room.

As we prayed to God for Him to be with us and for the money to be found, we heard a sudden "thud".

We opened our eyes, only to find that my secretary, Linda, had fallen down and hit the sideboard, sending all the files on it crashing down.

We thought she had fainted and one of us rushed to give her sugar water to drink.

When she revived, however, she was not hurt.

"Why are all of you surrounding me? What happened? I feel like I had fallen on feathery cushions," she said.

We then realised she had been slain by the Spirit in the presence of God, and felt reassured that even the concerning financial matter on hand would be resolved.

In the end, the auditors found that the $100,000 appeared to be "missing" in the accounts not because it was siphoned off, but because it was netted off by an exact corresponding outgoing expenditure. In other words, there was no misplaced funds.

This was a time when God visited us just when there was a big question of accountability hanging over our heads. It reminded us that we not only need to stay clean and honest, but to also be diligent with the administration of money matters.

Dot-Com Era

I consider my biggest shortcoming not my inability to count, but being a digital dinosaur in IT matters.

When the then MAS Chairman Mr Lee Hsien Loong, now the Prime Minister, wanted to roll out some Internet-based projects in line with the dot-com phase that the industry was going through, I was terrified.

Fear and panic overwhelmed my heart, and I did not feel ready or up to the task.

I was so scared at the prospect of having to lead or handle such high-tech projects that I once again contemplated leaving my job.

In the past, whenever I felt I could not perform or match up to what the job required, I would quit.

Two decades prior, I had also left my job at MAS when an internal restructuring exercise axed the bosses above me and I inadvertently became the number two in the department. I felt it would be too stressful for me to report to former Minister and Chairman of MAS Dr Goh Keng Swee and other ministers directly without having the cover of other senior management officials in between.

As I was praying over whether I ought to resign this time, God spoke to me through Psalm 131:1, part of which read: "I do not concern myself with great matters or things too wonderful for me."

I interpreted it as God urging me to not worry about the things that seemed too difficult for me, and instead continue doing what I was good at, whether it was my people skills or event management abilities.

So I knew that God had more plans for me at ABS. My time in ABS was not up yet.

I stayed to do my job faithfully, and let the experts handle that which I was not strong in or familiar with. The dot-com bubble eventually came and burst, and soon we found ourselves battling other giants.

Ai Boon is the face and voice of The Association of Banks in Singapore. In 2003, there was a major turning point when she asked me to attend a meeting where I learnt of a proposal for a debt counselling organisation, which would eventually be established as Credit Counselling Singapore (CCS).

The project was proposed by judges from the Subordinate Court and those promoting the project had neither banking experience nor had ever given a consumer loan. I was asked to take the lead on the initiative. A small team was formed to launch a pilot to test the waters.

Ai Boon was very prescient and spot-on with her sensing that it would be very difficult to get the ABS Council's approval from the start. There would be reservations about CCS having an anti-bank or anti-credit agenda. The beginning was therefore very painful as CCS had to deal with a group of 12 consumer banks which acted unilaterally with debtors and our debt repayment proposals were all on a best-effort basis.

However over time, with more experience of what CCS was doing and seeing positive results, the banks realised the usefulness of an independent and professional facilitator trying to restructure debts in a holistic manner with multiple bank creditors. Ai Boon did a splendid job in cajoling the banks to come together. She finally felt confident enough to get the CCS Debt Management Plan accepted and endorsed by the ABS Council. A revenue model based on the amount of debts recovered was also agreed on. CCS never looked back since then.

Ai Boon has strong convictions and determination to do what she thinks is right. She also has a deep and long institutional history and experience of working in ABS and understands what limitations there are. Her sense of timing and understanding of what and when she should or should not push is impeccable. Certainly the CCS project would have been sunk if she tried to get ABS Council's approval right at the onset.

It is not easy working in an organisation where the bosses change every two years. The fact is that she has persevered for so many decades and has provided a steady hand and wise counsel in the work of the Association.

In revealing her life story spanning five decades with its ups and downs, successes and failures, happiness and sorrows. she also shows us how her strong Christian faith has helped her find guidance and solace. This book will inspire many people in their spiritual quest.

Kuo How Nam

Honorary Adviser (2020–); Founder Member and first President (2004–2020),
Credit Counselling Singapore

APPOINTMENTS

ABS

The Association of Banks in Singapore (ABS) is establishing a Permanent Secretariat to provide continuing professional support and services to the ABS Council and wishes to recruit a high calibre individual to head the Permanent Secretariat as its:

DIRECTOR GENERAL

Salary negotiable plus attractive fringe benefits

The Director General will report to the ABS Council and, in the first instance, be responsible for organising the establishment of the Permanent Secretariat. The duties of the Director General will include the overall administration of the Permanent Secretariat; the planning and organising of projects and programmes in line with the objectives of the ABS; the implementation of policies and decisions of the ABS Council; the monitoring of developments affecting the banking industry; and the provision of relevant information, data and research to cater to the needs of ABS members. He will also have to liaise with various authorities and professional bodies.

The ideal candidate will be a person between 35 to 45 years of age with preferably a tertiary education or professional qualification. He should have a good overall exposure in banking with at least 10 years' experience in the banking industry. He must have the demonstrated ability to deal effectively at all levels coupled with good communication skills and leadership qualities.

This top position offers exciting and challenging opportunities to the right candidate to participate in the continuing growth and development of the banking industry in particular and Singapore as a financial centre in general. An attractive remuneration package consisting of salary and benefits will be negotiated with the selected candidate. As a guide, the salary should not be less than $70,000/- per annum.

Applications stating age, qualifications, experience, current earnings, contact telephone number and enclosing a recent photograph (non-returnable) should be addressed to:

The Chairman
The Association of Banks in Singapore
Level 2, PIL Building
140 Cecil Street
Singapore 0106

All applications will be treated with the strictest confidence. Application will close on October 24, 1981. Only candidates shortlisted will be notified.

The Straits Times' ad for the ABS Director General on 27 September 1981.

Source: *The Straits Times* © SPH Media Limited. Reprinted with permission.

Ai Boon, Senior Officer, Chung Khiaw Bank (CKB) promoting the bank's flagship children's coins bank savings account in 1970 with Lucy Kwok (in glossy *cheong sam*), Personal Assistant to Dato Lee Chee San, MD, CKB. Lucy later joined ABS as Ai Boon's deputy for more than a decade.

MAS official gets top post at bank association

[illegible]

Breaking news and fait accompli. 11 February 1982.

In 2018, Ai Boon met Soh Tiang Keng, the writer of the *The Straits Times* article which announced that she had accepted the top post at ABS before she made the decision herself.

The 1983 ABS AGM facilitated by the newly established permanent secretariat chaired by Chua Kim Yeow, President, DBS. L–R: Alan Ng Poh Meng, Deputy Chairman, UOB; Ai Boon, Director, ABS; Chua Kim Yeow; Lee Hee Seng, President, OUB.

Ai Boon, the newly appointed Director, ABS, hosted her guests at an ABS industry networking dinner in 1983 with her late husband Ong Hock Chye, former Deputy GM, OCBC (second from left).

MRS ONG-ANG AI BOON, Director, Association of Banks in Singapore:

THE woman I admire is Mrs Elizabeth Sam, the director of Simex. I worked with her years ago when she was with the Monetary Authority of Singapore. She's an amazing example of professionalism.

She taught me how a woman ought to conduct herself in a man's world — no asking for excuses or getting personal. And, equally important I think, she's also remained feminine without compromising her professionalism.

Central to her success is the fact that she knows her work inside out. She's so sharp! So if you're *really* smart, you'll make sure you know your onions just as well.

Ai Boon sharing her admiration for Mrs Elizabeth Sam, whom she worked with at MAS, in *The Straits Times* on 9 July 1989 in an interview about inspiring women leaders.

Ai Boon adds a personal touch with a thank you card to members of the ABS contingent, comprising staff from local and foreign banks at the National Day Parade 1990. They each received a personalised thank you card from Ai Boon for their participation which featured the ABS contingent marching past the Grandstand, City Hall.

The lean ABS team at the office in the MAS Building in the late 1980s.

L–R: Pearly, Sarah, Linda Phay (incumbent secretary), Ai Boon, Diane Chai, Abdul Razak Bin Kitan (driver for 30 years), Ng Soo Moi (accountant for almost four decades), Osman bin Shariff (despatch staff who served for 37 years), Lucy Kwok, Soh Wai Lin, Juliet.

As the industry grew, ABS enhanced and increased its staff strength.

The 40-strong ABS team in April 2023. Ai Boon (third from left); Shimah Ismail, COO (fourth from left); team leaders Ben Tay (second row, first left), Angeline Teng (first from left), Edmund Chong (second from left), Karen Li (seventh from left), Lisa Chow (eighth from left) and Bryan Lee (ninth from left); Linda Phay (fifth from left); Razak, who retired and re-engaged on contract (third row, first from left).

Dr Goh Keng Swee with the first batch of scholars of the Dr Goh Keng Swee Scholarship in 1992. The scholarship set up by the local financial and business community honours Dr Goh's role in fostering Singapore's economic development and growth as a reputable financial centre. Recipients of the scholarship are international students pursuing their tertiary education in Singapore.

L–R: Edward Wong Kar Ngai, Hong Kong; Wallace Leong Kin Kay, Malaysia; Dr Goh Keng Swee, Minister of Finance (1967–1970); Yang Yang, China; Oki Gunawan, Indonesia.

The annual ABS Lunar New Year lunch is a much-anticipated celebration for its members. Over the years, it has become an invaluable networking and bonding event that is carefully cultivated by the ABS team with zest and a touch of the unexpected.

2011: Ai Boon adding energy to the entertainment.

2017: Catching up with guests.

L–R: Kuo How Nam, Honorary Advisor, Founding President, Credit Counselling Singapore; William Lim, CEO, Credit Bureau Singapore; Ai Boon; Jeffrey Goh, CEO, NETS.

2017: Keeping up the festive cheer.

L–R: Ong Chong Tee, DMD, MAS; Ai Boon; Ravi Menon, MD, MAS; Wee Ee Cheong, Deputy Chairman & CEO UOB; Jacqueline Loh, DMD, MAS).

Senior bankers and Ai Boon band together for the President's Challenge at the ABS 30th Anniversary in 2003.

Jackson Tai, ABS Chairman and DBS CEO, drums up support for charity, while Judy Hsu, senior banker at Citibank Singapore, sings not for her dinner but for a good cause.

A conversation with Minister Mentor Lee Kuan Yew facilitated by Patrick Daniel, *Business Times* at the 2010 ABS 37th Annual Dinner.
Source: National Archives Singapore.

ABS celebrated its 40th anniversary in 2013, with 1,000 bankers from 28 banks coming together to plant 400 trees at a tree bank along Marina Coastal Drive, in collaboration with National Parks Board.

Tay Tien Guan, a regular speaker at the annual MoneySense programme, sharing at a seminar on "Understanding Loans and Avoiding the Debt Trap" in 2011.

ABS plays an important role in building regional collaboration and trust over the years through its support and active participation in the ASEAN Banking Council (ABC).

Chee Suan Lye, Executive Director, Association of Banks in Malaysia (second from left) with Ai Boon (first from left) and Peter Seah, EVP, OUB at the 15th ABC 1985.

Wong Nang Jang, EVP, OCBC (first from right) leading the Singapore delegation in a song at the social evening of the 27th ABC 1997 hosted by the Thai Bankers' Association. Supporting Nang Jang were Ng Kee Choe, President, DBS (first from left); Peter Seah, CEO, OUB; Ernest Wong, President, UOB.

The 18 members of the ABS Council (2019–2021) with Ai Boon at the 46th ABS AGM in 2019.

The annual Financial Crime Seminar (FCS), currently in its 19th edition, has been one of ABS' flagship events since it was organised in 2004. Supported by MAS and the Commercial Affairs Department of the Singapore Police Force, it aims to raise the financial sector's awareness of financial crime and has benefitted thousands who have attended the multi-day event.

Frank W. Abagnale, author of *Catch Me If You Can*, was a keynote speaker at the 2011 ABS FCS.

L-R: Jimmy Quek, MD, BCS; Ai Boon; Frank W. Abagnale; Tan Boon Gin, Head, CAD; Larry Lam, Consultant.

T Raja Kumar delivered the keynote address at the 2019 ABS FCS as Deputy Secretary (International and Training), Ministry of Home Affairs and Steering Group Member of the Financial Action Task Force, Singapore.

Recognising the finalists of the 12th edition of the ABS Service Excellence Champions 2018 from local and foreign banks at a ceremony attended by more than 7,000 bank staff.

PayNow launched at the ABS Annual Dinner 2017 by CEOs and senior management of the seven participating banks.

L–R: Jeremy Gwee, COO, HSBC; Judy Hsu, CEO, Standard Chartered; Piyush Gupta, CEO, DBS Group; Samuel Tsien, Group CEO, OCBC; Wee Ee Cheong, Deputy Chairman & CEO, UOB; Amol Gupte, ASEAN Head & Citi Country Officer, Citibank; Datuk Lim Hong Tat, CEO, MayBank; Ai Boon.

The 11 winners of the first Singapore Fintech Festival 2016 Hackathon with Sopnendu Mohanty, Chief Fintech Officer, MAS (first from left); Jacqueline Loh, DMD, MAS (fourth from left); Tharman Shanmugaratnam, Deputy Prime Minister and Chairman, MAS (sixth from left); Ravi Menon, MD, MAS (first from right); Ai Boon (fourth from right); Wee Ee Cheong, Deputy Chairman and CEO, UOB (sixth from right).

Since 2006, ABS and MAS have conducted six Industry Wide Exercises (IWEs) to prepare the financial sector for business continuity and build operational resilience. These exercises covered a wide range of scenarios, ranging from terrorist assaults to cyber security attacks and health emergencies, and helped the financial sector better manage crises such as the recent COVID-19 pandemic.

Networking at the IWE 2008 post-exercise cocktail reception.
L–R: Leo Mun Wai, Deputy MD, MAS; Ai Boon; Teo Swee Lian, Deputy MD, MAS; David Conner, CEO, OCBC.

A table-top exercise in progress at the Financial Industry Crisis Communications Exercise in 2016, a stream of the IWE, to fine-tune the communications flow.

The eventful 6th SFF appreciation dinner in November 2021 that sparked the writing of this book.

Seated L–R: Adeline Ho, Constellar; Pauline Wray, Boston Consulting Group; Sopnendu Mohanty, Chief Fintech Officer, MAS; Ai Boon; Navin Suri, CEO, Prescient.

Some of the people behind the story, including Cindy Yim, Seah Seng Choon, Peter Heng, Anu Suppiah, Ong Chin Ann and Albert Tan.

Dr Timothy Seow, acclaimed architect, whose Christian faith was revived after a health crisis, inspired Ai Boon on her faith journey.

Karen Kahrs (left), together with CT Lim and his wife, Ai Hoon. It was in the Lim's home that Ai Boon received Christ in October 1983.

Three generations became Christians consecutively: Ai Boon in 1983, followed by her mother a year later and her grandmother in 1985.

Ai Boon's mother, Mdm Sim, accepted the Lord in 1984.
Mdm Sim at her surprise 80th birthday party in 2005.

In 1985, Ai Boon's maternal grandmother, 84, became a Christian after her daughter, Mdm Sim, ministered to her. Five years later, Grandma went home to the Lord.

Ai Boon on vacation in 2013 in Vancouver in the home of Tze Lin, her elder son, and his wife MayAnn (first and second from left). Beside them are Ai Boon's daughter Shih Yi and her husband, Kevin Tong, and her younger son Tze Ru (second from right).

Ai Boon's younger son, Tze Ru, with Jing Yin and their children at East Coast Park in 2018.

Ai Boon with Dr Wong Yik Mun, her family doctor since 1975.

Chapter 11

Coming into My Own

On 30 November 1985, the beleaguered Pan-Electric Industries Limited (Pan-El), a marine salvage, hotel and property group, collapsed and was placed in receivership after having amassed huge debts totalling $453 million owed to 35 banks and $160 million worth of unfulfilled forward contracts.

The company's collapse resulted in the closure of the Singapore and Kuala Lumpur Stock Exchanges for three days that year in order to contain the fallout on heavily leveraged stockbroking firms. This marked the first and only time that the Singapore Stock Exchange had closed due to a trading emergency.

When the Pan-El crisis came, former DBS banker Mr Tay Tien Guan (fondly known as TG) was forced to sell all his shares when the stock markets reopened. His debts ballooned to $350,000 and by June 1986, he was served two judgement debts and had 17 creditors.

Desperate, TG made an unscheduled visit to my office one day with the intention of borrowing money from me.

I had first met him in 1985 when he participated in our ABS marching contingent at the National Day Parade. We became friends and I would share about my faith and the goodness of God over lunches with him. He had his own encounter with God later on and, subsequently, he became a believer.

On that fateful day when he suddenly walked into my office, I was not aware of the objective of his visit. As he was approaching me, a verse popped up in my mind and I said to him: "Put down your net and bring in the fish."

These words from Luke 5 were spoken by Jesus to Peter and the other fishermen who were fishing the whole night but had not caught anything. Upon meeting Jesus as they were returning to shore with their empty boats, he told them to go out again and let down their nets for a catch. Even though they knew there were no fishes, they nonetheless obeyed. Against logic, they eventually gathered so many fishes that their nets began to break and the boats began to sink.

After I gave him the verse, he made small talk with me and left. I was none the wiser about his state of mind or financial situation. It did not occur to me that he might have come to meet me for a reason, as I had assumed he was just dropping by for a visit.

Little did I know that, through the verse, God spoke to TG about his situation that day.

It was only a few years later, when TG invited me to a home meeting where he shared his testimony, that I realised the significance of what had taken place in my office that day. He had actually come to look for me in the office for financial help as he was in debt. Unknown to me, the Lord had given me those verses for TG to speak into the dire situation that he was facing.

During that time, he interpreted it as divine guidance to let go and let God take over by fully surrendering his predicament to God, instead of trying to fix it on his own by going around to borrow money.

"I did not open my mouth to borrow money and went before God to fully surrender and repent — no more borrowings, no more 4D, Toto, Big Sweep tickets and no more using my own strength, resources and wisdom," said TG when he recounted the incident.

He prayed to God for the strength to walk one day at a time if bankruptcy was the way forward for him. For the first time since the crisis occurred, the peace of God enveloped him. His irregular heart rate returned to normal and he found that he could sleep soundly once again.

Though he went through a difficult time in the next three-and-a-half years, miracles also began happening. God opened doors for him to secure three major projects and his mountain of debt was wiped out by 1989.

I have since learnt that it does not matter whether the word I received from God made sense in the situation; my role is just to relay it and trust God to do the rest.

Beyond being debt-free, TG was enabled to use his former area of brokenness to now equip others in financial literacy. He eventually left his job at DBS Bank and went on to spend the next 17 years as a fee-based financial adviser. When he went into the training and coaching business in 2007, ABS engaged him to be a speaker for the national financial literacy programme MoneySense as he had first-hand experience of getting into and out of debt. For over five years, he taught students and working adults in the polytechnics, universities, police force, army camps and various organisations how to understand loans and avoid the debt trap.

I am amazed by his testimony. God not only used me to guide TG, but also used him to return to the community and bless others by sharing his experience of being an overcomer. We remain good friends to this day.

Rising Up to the Occasion

After 20 years of leading ABS under the training and guidance of local Chairmen, whom I learnt much from, the season shifted into one where I was thrust into a higher level of leadership.

Until the late 1990s, all the big four Singapore banks — UOB, DBS, OCBC and OUB — had CEOs who were Singaporeans. Under the leadership of then Finance Minister Mr Lee Hsien Loong, who was also Chairman of MAS, there was a pronounced shift to open up the banking sector. We needed to be more open to compete with large global banks and realise Singapore's vision to become an international financial centre.

Thus, more foreign banks were admitted and more foreign CEOs were engaged in the local banks. The thinking behind it was that the foreign talent would bring in different mindsets and dynamics that could grow Singapore's presence and influence in global banking.

DBS was the first to pivot in 1998. They engaged Mr John Olds, an American, and he helmed the bank till 2001. He was later succeeded by Mr Philippe Paillart, who was French, and subsequently by other Americans such as Mr Jackson Tai and Mr Richard Stanley. OCBC also engaged its first foreign CEO in 1998: Mr Alex Au who was from Hong Kong. Au was succeeded by Mr David Conner, an American, and then Mr Samuel Tsien from Hong Kong took over. Until then, all the previous CEOs of DBS and OCBC had been stalwart Singaporean bankers.

I had the opportunity and privilege to work with a few of the foreign CEOs from DBS and OCBC since 2001 as the ABS Chairmanship was rotated amongst the banks once every two years. The first foreign ABS Chairman I worked with was Alex Au in 2001 when the Chairmanship rotated to OCBC.

As he was not a Singaporean and relatively new to the affairs of the Association, I had to step up to provide advisory services. These included giving recommendations on how different stakeholders should work together in the local banking scene, as well as advice on other corporate protocols unique to our cultural context.

The foreign CEOs entrusted me with the administration and management of ABS. I took charge and made decisions when dealing with its various committees. As they encouraged rigorous debate and a robust exchange of ideas, I began learning how to say "no" whenever the situation called for it.

This period marked a turning point for me as it was the time when I rose up and gave back by tapping on my years of experience in steering the ABS ship under the guidance of previous Chairmen who were long-time Singaporean bankers.

Championing the Needs of the Voiceless

In 2002, a State Courts judge called me at the office. A mutual friend had referred me to her as she and four other judges were trying to find a solution to help over-indebted families and alleviate the negative impact that such financial strain had on families.

Over lunch, the judges told me that they were seeing more creditors take legal action against individuals whose debt woes had overturned their personal lives and families — much like the sob stories depicted in the 1998 local box-office hit, *Money No Enough*. But unlike the movie's protagonists, who resolved their money troubles by winning a $100,000 windfall in an obstacle race, these Singaporeans had little luck getting out of the debt pit.

Many families were breaking up, the judges explained, when the breadwinners became bankrupt and lost their jobs. If there was an arrangement to enable them to repay loans in smaller amounts and keep their jobs, families would have a higher chance of staying intact. Their struggles moved my heart.

Singapore needed a credit counselling scheme and we could learn from the UK and Canadian schemes which permit debtors to repay their debts in small amounts monthly, they explained.

We all agreed that having such a scheme locally could provide financial advice for these individuals to avoid bankruptcy, represent them by negotiating a reasonable debt restructuring plan with the banks and help them budget for a debt-free future. However, having such an arrangement would be administratively too cumbersome for banks to handle.

I prayed about it. I was convicted to do something about this matter when God reminded me of His commands in Proverbs 31:8–9:

"Open your mouth for the speechless,
In the cause of all who are appointed to die.
Open your mouth, judge righteously,
And plead the cause of the poor and needy."

I knew those in debt did not have a voice for themselves as they could have been under the control of eight or nine creditors. They needed people to 'open their mouths' to speak up for them.

There was just one big issue holding me back from driving this — credit counselling did not yet fall under ABS' mandate. The thought of coming up with a proposal to try to convince Council members to give their stamp of approval for this project seemed too overwhelming.

I was really convicted that setting up such a service would be the right thing to do, yet I did not want to run the risk, no matter how small the chances, of the Council turning down my recommendation if I was not convincing enough. So, I just went ahead to do it in my personal capacity by tapping on my own network of contacts. However, I did caution the judges that this was not yet an ABS project. I figured that if it became successful and I could prove its value to the Council's banks, then it was more likely to be supported thereafter.

The first step was getting seed finance in order to get the right people with the relevant expertise on board.

I called on Mr Tan Soo Nan, a former Managing Director at DBS with whom I had worked closely and who was the CEO of Singapore Pools then, to provide some financial support. Upon hearing more about the expected benefits of the project, he was convinced and seeded $100,000.

I also called up Mr Kuo How Nam, a retired banker who used to specialise in consumer banking at DBS and then OUB, to join a meeting with the several judges.

He had retired at the age of 53 and had been enjoying life in a slower-paced role as the Chairman of Creation Media, a publisher of magazines like *Senior Life* which was targeted at senior citizens.

The last thing he expected was to take up a new job at the meeting. Yet when he turned up, he found the proposition of setting up a credit counselling service deeply meaningful and intriguing.

He took up the job on a volunteer basis and became the President and first founding member of the Credit Counselling Singapore (CCS).

I also roped in Ms Tan Huey Min, a former ABS staff who had interned at a credit counselling centre in the United States while doing her master's degree in consumer and family economics.

She has a heart of gold and I thought she was the best fit for the job at CCS. She was keen and willingly left her job as a polytechnic lecturer to become CCS' first employee. She was sent to understudy the schemes in the UK and Canada. Today, she heads the CCS.

Uphill Battle

It was no cushy job at the non-profit CCS, with How Nam, Huey Min and an administrative staffer huddled in a cramped, 200 sq ft room that Singapore Pools provided rent-free.

Funding was a big problem. This was a charity that helped indebted people and did not have the emotive appeal of charities for sick children or the disabled. It was also hampered by the perception that its clients were indebted for ignoble reasons like gambling or spendthrift habits. CCS initially relied on donations raised from individuals and charitable organisations.

CCS also lacked any standing or clout among the creditor banks with whom it sought to negotiate. During the six-month pilot, CCS struggled to gain consensus with multiple lenders — which could number six or 12 or more — for its relief and restructuring proposals.

To overcome the banks' hesitancy about working with CCS, I arranged for the creditor banks to meet with CCS at the ABS office, lending legitimacy to CCS' Debt Management Programme proposals. I urged the various banks to play ball and comply in unity by agreeing to a set of repayment terms across the board so that debtors could get reduced repayment amounts at a lowered interest rate from all the participating banks.

How Nam's deep expertise in unsecured credit and his network of contacts also smoothed the way for CCS to pull in volunteers to serve and gain recognition for its work.

The initial pilot project encouraged How Nam and his team to take the plunge to register a society in 2004 to formalise the scheme. It persevered with its efforts to engage the consumer banks and after two years, the banks began to see the advantages of having a facilitator to restructure all consumer debts. I then managed to persuade the ABS Council to formally adopt CCS's Debt Management Programme and to provide a grant to be shared by the major consumer banks to help with their finances for two years. The continued success of CCS's Debt Management Programme finally persuaded the Council to set up a formal fee arrangement where CCS would obtain a small token fee based on the amount of debts recovered. This provided the foundation and stability for CCS's continued operations till this day.

By 2022, the service had counselled over 35,000 individuals. It would become a trusted partner to ABS and the banks, as well as MAS, in helping indebted individuals restructure their debts, organising public education programmes and administering the Repayment Assistance Scheme (which helps individuals meet a new cap on borrowing limits). During the recent COVID period, it also assisted over-indebted customers to tide over their difficult financial situations.

Being able to do something in my position to influence outcomes that are for the better good of vulnerable consumers energises me.

I know that when the motive is rightly aligned with His Word and will, such as when we have compassion for others, God will provide the right people and resources to see the idea to fruition.

Part 4

Strength in Weaknesses

Chapter 12

A Hundred Red Roses

In 2001, my 55th birthday fell on a Monday.

As I was about to conduct my usual Monday fellowship in the office during lunchtime, my husband suddenly walked in with a huge bouquet of 100 red roses. The card that came with the flowers read: "Totally in love with you, Hubby."

I knew then that he was actually not in love with 'me'. Eighteen years prior, my husband had seriously proposed a separation as he found living with me unbearable. So I remarked to him that it was the 'Christ in me' that he was in love with, as I could not have transformed so much by myself.

What was even more surprising and amazing was how he proceeded to read Proverbs 31 as an ode to me. I was overwhelmed with emotion when he got to verses 28–29:

"Her children arise and call her blessed;
her husband also, and he praises her:
'Many women do noble things,
but you surpass them all.'"

My deputy, Lucy Kwok, who was present and witnessed everything that day, also teared. Unknown to my husband, it had always been my secret desire for him to use those verses to describe me.

I had told God of this desire of my heart, and I had also shared it with Lucy some years back. She remembered and wept in joy for me when she heard it as she knew how much it meant to me.

It had been my goal to try to become a Proverbs 31 woman simply because I realised I was the exact opposite of such a woman.

I used to wear the pants at home and struggled with submitting to my husband's authority.

One day, I was on the road when I heard a sermon about how Jezebel usurped control from her husband, King Ahab, and manipulated him. Her behaviour displeased God and she came to a gory end. Convicted that I also had the Jezebel spirit of intimidation, domination and manipulation, I ran into the office and cried out to Lucy in horror: "Lucy, I am a witch! I am a witch!"

I was a witch because I realised the spirit of Jezebel is linked to witchcraft, and I purposed in my heart that anything that is not of God in my life must be removed.

In the past, it was hard for me submit to my husband because I felt I was in the right. Therefore, it felt unfair if I had to compromise on my views, opinions or decisions simply because God has placed him above me as the head of the household.

However, that conflict within myself was resolved when God gently urged me to simply obey His Word, which called for me to submit to my husband. By then, it was easier for me to obey God and submit to my husband whom I had learnt to appreciate much more because of all that He had done in my life.

When I obeyed Him, I realised that it was in His immense wisdom to establish an order in His kingdom and in the family unit as 1 Corinthians 11:3 puts it: The head of every man is Christ, and the head of the woman is man, and the head of Christ is God.

This does not make the woman inferior to man, but it is simply a divine order for things to work well. For instance, when we build the roof on top of the pillars and foundation of a house, it does not mean the roof is the most important part of the house. All parts have a distinct function and, if one is removed, the entire structure can collapse.

Whether we are a man or woman, we are all called to submit to each other in the fear of the Lord.

Thus, I was extremely elated when my husband read out Proverbs 31 to me during my 55th birthday celebration. Part of the joy was due to my husband witnessing and testifying of God's work in my life. But most of it was because it felt like I was receiving a good report card from God.

I had passed the test. However, I knew there was still more refining and sanctifying to be done.

The Test of Jealousy

Another test that I was put through in our relationship was experiencing and understanding jealousy.

In all my past relationships, there was no reason for jealousy. My self-protective pride made sure that I was the one walking out on others before they could walk out on me.

So, I never knew what jealousy felt like, until it was provoked not by a woman, but a man.

My husband had retired and come to befriend Mr Albert Tan — then the IT service provider who installed the LAN system in ABS — through me. Previously, Albert and his family had also received Christ through my office fellowship.

It was clear why my husband and Albert hit it off immediately. Albert was a wonderful conversationalist and good company to my husband, and he treated my husband like the father he had never had.

My husband was a gadget freak, and Albert ran an electronics store at Funan shopping mall. Both of them would go crazy over the latest gadgets and enjoyed flying drones together. As my husband had retired by then, he would often spend his day hanging out with Albert at his store. They also had the similar hobbies of flying remote control planes, rearing birds and fish as pets.

Slowly, I began to realise that I was jealous of their close relationship. I felt strong feelings of irritation every time my husband looked for Albert, or whenever I found that my husband was yet again with Albert when I asked about his whereabouts.

Often, my husband would also follow Albert in his van as he did his delivery rounds islandwide to fulfil his store orders. Once when they were making deliveries in the Woodlands area, my husband told Albert that he felt like eating Indian *rojak* at a particular stall at Waterloo Street. Without hesitation, Albert drove him all the way there from Woodlands to satisfy his craving. After lunch, they drove back to Woodlands to complete the deliveries for the day.

When I heard about it, I was really impressed by the depth of Albert's love for his friend. So, this is what love is — a person would do almost anything for a loved one. It softened my heart and I learnt how to love and serve my husband better.

I was set free from my feelings of jealousy when I started to recognise and acknowledge such feelings. I did not act on those feelings because I saw that it was a beautiful friendship between my husband and Albert, whom we viewed as our "godson".

However, my experience of having those strong feelings of jealousy helped me to truly be able to empathise with those to whom I minister, especially spouses who have the same struggles. Being able to put myself in their shoes prevented me from being self-righteous and talking down to them.

The friendship between Albert and my husband was so close that he told me to call Albert to our house immediately when he felt breathless one night in 2006. Albert rode with him in the ambulance to the hospital that night.

Going Home

Back in 1996, my husband was given a second lease on life when he suffered a heart attack. I had pleaded with the Lord then, to allow me more time to joyfully serve him as a wife. My prayer was answered.

In the next decade, there would be three more occasions when my husband would slip into unconsciousness. It happened twice in Tokyo when we visited our younger son who was working there at that time, and once in Mount Elizabeth Hospital.

Each time it happened, I would pray and not stop doing so until he became conscious. When my husband awoke, he would share with me that he felt very peaceful and saw a bright light during the time when he was unconscious.

But on one of those occasions, he told me that he wanted to walk towards the Light but he did not follow through with it because he felt he had to return to me as I still needed him. Quoting from Philippians 1:23–24, he said he was "torn between the two: (he) desired to depart and be with Christ, which is better by far; but it is more necessary for (me) that (he) remain in the body." So, he returned.

When my husband was admitted into hospital in 2006, I was not too perturbed. He had even asked me to bring his Bible reading glasses to him.

Little did I realise that he would never come out of the Intensive Care Unit. His vital signs plunged due to complications arising from his heart and kidneys, and he died two days later.

I took his death calmly as I knew where he was going and that we would meet again one day. I was thankful that the Lord had already extended his life by10 years, as it had been a decade since he had had his heart surgery.

Yet when the funeral wake was ongoing, I suddenly felt alone and told God: "Now, I don't have my husband to talk to and discuss matters with."

The Lord responded to me with the verses in Isaiah 54:5, and He told me: "I will be your husband."

That reminded me of the time, some 35 years ago, when Ms Karen Kahrs, a lady from my Thursday fellowship group, described to me the dream she had of me.

In her dream, she was at my wedding, and she was wondering who I was marrying as she had also seen my husband in the audience witnessing the wedding. I was getting married to another man, she recalled, and there was so much joy in the atmosphere.

I knew then, that the man in her dream was Christ.

After my husband's death, I continued to look to God for all my needs.

A Suit Made of Teflon

Following the death of my husband, I grieved. With my spirit down and heavy, I withdrew from most social activities and kept to myself. I did not go for group gatherings, parties or even church camps for a while.

One Saturday, Senior Elder Wee Tiong Howe from my church called me and asked me to join a church meeting. He told me that Russel

Sage, a prophet, was in town and he would be speaking at the meeting. Though I felt like staying at home, I obliged and dutifully went to church.

At the meeting, the prophet started speaking but suddenly stopped and singled me out. He began his message to me by saying: "I see you in a business suit..." That sentence immediately caught my attention and raised my faith in his prophetic word because I would usually wear a suit to the office, though he would not have known it as I was casually dressed at that meeting.

"... and your suit is made of Teflon," he continued. The interpretation was that God has given me a 'non-stick' suit where the words, criticism or praise of others would not stick on me but fall off me easily.

I was glad for the word given to me as it was crucial for me not to be easily offended or take things personally in the course of my work, where ABS often functioned as an honest broker and middleman. I needed to know my identity in the Lord, and stay objective and professional in what I do.

To me, having a Teflon suit means that I would not be afraid of Man as I trusted God with all that I needed to do at work. It was different from being the crab that I saw myself as — having a hard outer shell of self-protection as a façade to protect the soft inner tissues of all my insecurities.

With God's assurance that He would equip me with a Teflon suit at work, and be my husband to meet all my other needs, I found the strength to continue to conduct the Monday and Thursday fellowships without fail, even after my husband's death.

In addition to these two fellowships, I also took over the Wednesday lunchtime fellowship — that my husband used to helm at the High Street Centre for workers in the vicinity — for several years.

All these fellowships had a strong and uplifting impact on me. I was ministered by the presence of God, His Word and His leading, and these weekly doses of 'fresh manna' (daily bread) would refresh and sustain me for rest of the week.

I am delighted to contribute my endorsement of this book chronicling Ai Boon's eventful journey over the years at the helm of The Association of Banks in Singapore.

I first met with Ai Boon back in 2008 when I was Chief Executive of the Casino Regulatory Authority. I was immediately struck by her energy, passion and zeal to serve.

Ai Boon has been the guiding light at ABS these past 40 years and has made a significant difference to the banking and wider community through her many contributions. In more recent years, I had the opportunity to feature as a keynote speaker at ABS' Annual Financial Crime Seminar and, in the course of our interactions at the conference and over dinner, gained a deeper understanding of Ai Boon and her motivation, and felt her deep commitment to serve in order to further God's work.

She has exemplified how one can serve well through marketplace ministry. I hope that Ai Boon's leadership journey, ethos and candid sharing will inspire many to give of themselves and their talents for a higher purpose.

T. Raja Kumar

Chapter 13

From Tigress to Cat

I was a difficult boss at work. As a workhorse who not only expected much of myself, I also came down hard on my staff.

Staff who did not seem to have any common sense grated on my nerves badly. I was fastidious with the work that went out, as I felt it would reflect badly on the Association and myself if it did not meet certain expectations.

As a result, I became a micromanager — an impatient and bad-tempered one at that.

Once, my secretary went for an operation and I had to find a replacement. To my dismay, I learnt that the assigned staff member did not want to work with me because of my reputation for being quick-tempered.

The rejection hit me hard. It felt so painful that I was left reeling from literal pain, and had no choice but to take emergency leave that day. I went home and wept in my room. As I cried, the song "I'll Never

Let Go of Your Hand" happened to be playing in the background.

I was ministered by its lyrics: "Embarrassed by your weaknesses ... No matter what may happen, child / I'll never let go of your hand / I know you've been forsaken / By all you've known before / When you've failed their expectations / They frown and close the door."

It felt as though God had entered my bedroom. I was sure He was speaking to me as I had previously told Him that I would put my hand in His and He must not let go of my hand as I did not trust myself. It was as if He was reassuring me that He was still holding on to my hand, even in a time like that. His intimate presence in the room healed me of the rejection that I felt.

Unfortunately, my notorious reputation continued to precede me. There was once when I was invited by Ms Cindy Yim, a former officer at the MAS who used to report to me, to her wedding dinner. But I was unable to attend it. Shortly after, I met her again at a Christian lunchtime function and she joked with me that some of my ex-staff at MAS had chosen not to attend her wedding after knowing that I may have been there.

Said in jest, her comment was true but it still hurt me. As I sat at the table talking to God about it and licking my wounds, another woman came. She squatted down to my level and told me how much the testimony of God's work in my life, which I had just shared, ministered to her.

My spirits were lifted up, and I realised God had been kind in sending the other woman over with a word of encouragement after I was left hurting by the comments of another. I now know that people may dislike me because of my fleshly self, but God is still able to use me as long as I chose to die to my old self daily and walk the talk.

High Turnover Rate

As I was a difficult boss to work with, there were a number of years when ABS experienced a high turnover rate.

In 2011, a few of my staff members decided to leave after I promoted an employee over another long-serving senior staff member. They were in the same clique as the senior staff member and had left the Association in protest.

I stuck to my decision as I felt that the employee who was promoted had deserved it more, though the other senior staff member had been around longer. In hindsight, I should have given the senior staff member some recognition as well, as a form of appreciation.

The timing of their departure coincided with an employee who needed to be away from the office for some time and another who had just retired. This meant that we were down to half of the staff strength.

With only half of the team left, the employee whom I had just promoted came running to me in panic, asking me how we would cope with the workload.

That was when I remembered that God had previously made it possible for me to operate with a lean team. I shared with her the story.

In the earlier days, I found myself shorthanded when several members of my staff had to take emergency leave, including my secretary who went for surgery to remove gallstones.

I prayed to God, bemoaning to Him that I did not have enough people to help me run the Association.

Interestingly, the next two weeks were the quietest period I have experienced in my decades of working at the Association.

The phone hardly rang and no new projects came in. Thus, I was able to cope with the work, despite being shorthanded.

This time, I went to God again to ask for His help with a more dire manpower situation.

I started reading Psalms, from Chapter 18 onwards, and it was only when I read Psalms 33, that I felt Him speaking to me through these verses: "From heaven the Lord looks down and sees all mankind ... No king is saved by the size of his army; no warrior escapes by his great strength ... But the eyes of the Lord are on those who fear him, on those whose hope is in his unfailing love, to deliver them from death and keep them alive in famine."

I felt God reassuring me that He would see us through this tight manpower situation. I shared this with the newly promoted staff member who was troubled over the departure of her colleagues. She felt better and agreed to press on to do the work with me, as it may take some time for new workers to be hired.

After a few months, she remarked to me: "I felt as if there were people working with me; the work seemed to get done faster."

Eventually, we managed to finish all the work smoothly, and even had time left to spare before the year ended.

Over the years, though a number of staff left ABS because they could not stand me, God provided me with the right people at the right time to enable my team and me to do the job well.

About two decades ago, for instance, we pioneered an annual financial crime seminar. In the early days, it was quite a challenge persuading people, who have their own full-time jobs, to be part of a committee to organise such a seminar, and then to invite the relevant subject experts to be the speakers.

Having to put the seminar together felt tiresome and overwhelming, and I was close to throwing in the towel. That was when an Alternate Council member, Mr Michael Young, then COO of HSBC, stepped in and gave me a timely word of advice.

"No, don't stop doing this, the industry needs it," he urged me.

It was just a few words of wise advice, but it was enough to motivate me and give me a second wind.

At that time, anti-money laundering (AML) and terrorism financing were pretty new and nascent, and it was important for us to do what was needed to create awareness for the industry.

Michael's reminder of its importance energised me and imbued in me the passion to continue laying the foundations for the seminar.

It has since become an ABS flagship annual event — now in its 19th year, organised with the support of MAS, Commercial Affairs Department and the S Rajaratnam School of International Studies — that drew more than a thousand attendees in 2022, including thought leaders with expertise in the area.

On another occasion, I was pulling my hair out trying to write a script for an AML video as I felt it was not up to the mark. At a meeting with the banks in the ABS conference room, I looked over the video script in despair. Mr Dominic Nixon, a partner from PricewaterhouseCoopers (PwC), came over and offered his help. He roped in a colleague from his team to help me with the script, and I am still grateful to him for that favour.

I believe that these incidents show God's provision and favour. Even as I agreed to stay on to do the work at ABS in obedience to His will, I believe He was faithful in providing for all my needs, especially when difficult challenges arose.

Others have also told me that I have a knack for picking the right people to work with me in the Committees; it's true. I will selectively work with those who are willing and able. I also have a core team of faithful and loyal staff who have stuck with me for decades, even when others come and go.

For example, my current secretary Linda has been working with me for 40 years. I hired her for the job, though she was not very proficient in English and did not have any stenography skills unlike another better qualified candidate who had also applied for the job. She turned out to be a dedicated and hardworking employee, a good friend and a prayer warrior with whom I would pray alongside regularly.

Several others in my core staff team during the early years — Lucy Kwok, Diane Chai, Wang Meng Day, Ng Soo Moi and Pamela See — were my loyal lieutenants who understood me and worked with me for decades. I am grateful to them for having stood by me through the years.

ABS' current COO, Shimah binte Ismail, first came in as a clerical officer in 1996, but she was ambitious. After a few years, she wanted me to train her to become a project officer. I discouraged her as I felt she lacked the domain knowledge and skills.

One day, she volunteered to help me solve a problem on hand by coming up with a voucher system to better account for petty cash claims. I noticed that she was intelligent and resourceful, and began to groom her in logistics and event management. She excelled in managing the operations of the office and had a good understanding of the relevant protocols required. Today, she has risen to become our Chief Operating Officer.

Despite having these stellar employees, building a strong and effective secretariat team at ABS has been challenging. For many years, it was difficult attracting and retaining talent. This was not due to ABS having stringent requirements for domain knowledge and subject matter expertise; what was required to be effective at ABS was simply to have a good work ethic; administrative, organisational and interpersonal skills; as well as a dollop of common sense.

Instead, many young talents typically had ambitions that exceeded what the Association could offer. For the ones that did join, they often cut their teeth at the Association for a few years and then left for greener pastures, often at one of our member banks.

I did not stop them from leaving as I understood that the career opportunities at the Association were limited. In the same vein, I also do not poach employees who are happily engaged in their jobs elsewhere, as the responsibility of meeting their expectations would be too much to bear.

One side effect of this natural churn was that when a key officer resigned, I would have to step in to fill the gap. I did not mind that much as I was a very hands-on boss and I love the work.

'Management Theories' for Parenting and Leadership

The way I manage my staff is influenced by what God revealed to me when I was seeking Him for wisdom in parenting my children.

When I first came to Christ, one of the first questions I asked Him during my quiet time was: "How do I raise my children?" I wanted to raise my children His way.

He showed me a railway yard, similar to what I used to see at the former Tanjong Pagar railway station, having travelled by train many times with my mother to her hometown in Kuala Lumpur, Malaysia, in my growing up years.

The yard had several railway tracks.

"For each of your children, I have already built a railway track," He said to me. "If you don't help him or her find that track, and instead build your own track for them, or if they are to build their own, they will derail."

I realised that God was pointing out to me that He has placed a destiny and path for each one of us, and our task as parents or leaders is simply to guide them in order to help them discover it.

Therefore, as a boss I try not to simply push people to do what I want them to do. If I notice that they have certain talents or giftings that are not suited to the current role they are in, I would reshuffle them so that they can find the track that God has already planned for them.

Another 'management theory' that God Himself taught me was in examining the motives of my heart when I lead others.

I was a tiger mum who continually pressured my children to study hard.

One time, I felt God asking me: "Why are you doing this (pressuring them)?"

My answer of "it's for their sake" was just at the tip of my tongue, but I held it back. I knew that was not the truth that God was seeking.

As I dug deeper within, the real answers started to surface.

"If they do well, I would boast about them. If they don't do well, it would inconvenience me and I would lose face."

I realised then that pushing my children to study was not an act of love. It was more for myself, out of my own self-centredness.

Similarly, when I push my staff in the office, I try to be aware of my underlying motive. At times, I was overly perfectionist about the work done because of my own fear and vanity of not meeting external performance standards. Such consciousness helps me to be less self-serving, and to pull back if I find that I have gone too far.

I see my staff not as a resource to be used. The office must be a safe space, conducive to their flourishing. At the same time, I am also refined at the workplace. Even those with whom I found it difficult to work, I would still retain them, guiding them along and deeming them divine instruments to change my behaviour with grace. Some stayed on, while others chose to leave on their own accord.

For example, there was a particular external work partner whom my staff hated to work with as he was not punctual for meetings and did not deliver on his deadlines. My officers would complain about him not picking up calls and dragging his feet on projects. Eventually, they came to my office one day to tell me that they would not work with him.

However, I felt compassion for him, and had a burden to protect him instead of removing the project from him. Yet I knew it was not fair for my staff to have to continue to work with him just because I felt a burden for him.

I had to take responsibility if I wanted him to stay on and keep the project. I relieved my staff of their duties to work with him and told them I would take over the project and work with him directly.

It was not easy. Apart from telling him about areas that he could improve, I also took my complaints to the Lord by writing to Him copiously in my journal.

Instead of harbouring critical emotions in blaming and accusing the other party of not performing, I needed to see my own errors of not bearing the fruit of patience, gentleness and self-control.

Slowly, God honoured my obedience and sincerity.

The work partner changed for the better. The two ABS officers, who used to have trouble working with him, began having compassion for him and volunteered to continue working with him for other projects.

I learnt that when we take on the Lord's yoke, His "yoke is easy, and (His) burden is light" (Matthew 11:30).

There was another staff member whom I had hired who became "a thorn in (my) flesh".

I had heard that she had left her job because her former bosses constantly scolded her, but I took her in anyway because she had the relevant experience.

She was technically competent, but she could not sync with the Association's culture. There were many times when I became really upset with her, yet I told myself that I, as a Christian, cannot behave like her ex-bosses.

Twice, in meetings, I was so angry that I scolded her for doing the job poorly. When I realised what I had done, I went over to hug her in the middle of the meeting. The onlookers were taken aback, and they heard me clarifying with her that I was upset at the work done, but it was not meant to be taken personally.

One day, an external work partner who had worked with her at previous ABS events came up to me and blurted out: "Boss, what did you do to her? She has totally changed and become so humble and polite now."

I realised that when staff come to work with me, the experience must be a restorative and beneficial one, not only for myself, but for them as well.

Through the genuine joy I take in helping my staff flourish, perhaps this tigress boss has been slowly evolving into a tamer house cat.

Chapter 14

The Gift of Hospitality

Having some degree of emotional intelligence (EQ) was not only helpful in managing my staff, but it also accentuated the gift of hospitality with which I believe God has blessed me.

There is a common refrain among bankers in the industry that go: "When ABS invites, just go, you will find the best food."

Whether it is ASEAN meetings, annual events or conferences that ABS organises, we take much pride in serving our partners and stakeholders with the best service and experience.

At our past events, we have brought in live stations where guests could enjoy the experience of seeing food cooked on the spot. Menus are specially curated to have a good balance and variety between cooking styles and type of food. For instance, a meal cannot feature too many braised or fried dishes, spicy elements or similar types of meats. Door gifts are specially selected and not run-of-the-mill.

Even the size and type of crockery used, I stipulated, need to be appropriate for the quantity of food being served as the precision of presentation is key to having a 'wow' experience.

The timing of each dish being served is also important. Once during an ABS industry event when the serving of the food was substantially delayed, I personally went into the hotel kitchen to check on them and chase them.

In the early days, ABS was one of the first organisations that started the practice of personalising seating plans by placing name cards in front of each guest on the table to facilitate better networking (though it is common practice now).

Whenever we have committee or Council meetings, I would make it a point to get special treats for the members. Often, I get ideas from the latest food reviews in the newspapers. Once, for instance, I read about some delicious *vadai* made by an Indian couple from Bedok and our staff made a beeline to get them and have them served at our meetings.

Food preferences of our work partners and guests are also conscientiously noted. I would notice that a particular council member eats fungus but not mushrooms, and that another member really enjoyed the curry puffs from a certain store, and try to serve them what they like.

I look into such details to personalise our service to the members because many of the bankers and partners who pitch in to do the Association's work do so on top of their full-time jobs. We want them to feel our genuine appreciation for their contribution and to have fun while doing such 'extra-curricular' work.

An ABS Chairman once suggested that we outsource the organisation and logistics of such event management work as it could be too laborious and time-consuming for ABS to organise all of its events by itself.

We tried doing so, but it did not work out. The event management companies were bound by contract terms and could not provide any extras or variation that we sometimes needed on the spot to create a memorable experience for our guests. Sometimes, they acceded to the requests but charged much more for them and it became expensive. Even though we held our events at certain hotels fairly frequently, we were also unable to develop a closer relationship with the hotel staff as the event management company was our middleman.

Eventually, we decided to take on the organising of the events ourselves. This gave us greater autonomy to curate a special experience for our guests without blowing the budget. Over time, we also developed good working relationships with the hotels and chefs, who were excited to experiment with us and create new dishes for us that were not in the usual à la carte menu.

To this day, all ABS events are still organised by our own in-house events team. I am very proud of the team for continually honing their event organising skills.

The Heart of Hospitality

We can offer service in an efficient and technically competent way, but without true hospitality coming from the heart, it will seem cold.

That's the difference between hospitality and service. Hospitality is not about fawning upon others, but humbling oneself to understand and meet the needs of others.

I recall an occasion in my earlier days when we had a family barbecue at my home. I had prepared the garlic butter and two of my sisters were tasked with buying the French loaf for us to make toasted garlic bread. Instead of the classic French loaf, they came with the usual loaf of sliced bread. I flew into a rage, as it was only appropriate to use French loaf to make the garlic bread on the barbecue grill, not sliced bread.

My siblings were aghast and critical of me for being so particular. To them, the sliced bread was still bread. Yet I was annoyed that they did not take the trouble to look for the French loaf when they could not find it at the first bakery that they went to. They compromised and I would not have it.

They felt that I was being too fastidious about the precision of presentation, but what bothered me was the heart behind the matter. It seemed as if they did not care much for it.

While I may have a point — that hospitality involves focusing on the little details because it shows a care and consideration for others — the way I exploded in response to my sisters was wrong because it did not exemplify the grace of God.

It took time — a daily denying and dying to self over the next 40 years — to hone my hospitality skills that needed to be refined with patience, gentleness and self-control.

To me, true hospitality not only involves showing grace when events of the day do not go as planned, it also requires me to search deeper within to examine my true intention and motive.

God showed me that my ability to put out a lavish feast for my guests was of no import if I was doing it for the wrong reasons.

I remember the time when my family went on a holiday to New Zealand and Australia with two other families in 1983. I was a new Christian then.

We all stayed in an apartment at Gold Coast and I had planned to cook a meal for the group before we returned home to Singapore. In the kitchen, I laid out all the food — beef, chicken, noodles, seafood and vegetables — that I had purchased from the supermarket. I was about to start cooking when I heard the Lord ask me: "Why are you cooking?"

Knowing that He was trying to tell me something, I searched my heart earnestly for the real reason why I wanted to cook for everyone that night. Then, I answered Him honestly: "Lord, it's because I want to show off."

That was such a revelation to me. I knew how I would enjoy the accolades and compliments that I would receive from the guests.

After I had received Jesus in my heart, I loved these occasions when God would speak to me and confront me with hidden matters of my true self. The aim was to set me free of self-centredness and self-importance which made me competitive and selfish.

I repented and apologised to God. That evening, I cancelled the dinner and used the food to prepare meals for my own family over the next couple of days.

Subsequently, when the church needed food for some charity and fellowship events, I went back to God to ask Him for permission to cook. This time, I told Him I was cooking out of necessity to help out and not to "show off", and I was given the green light to go ahead.

I place so much emphasis on hospitality because it has been key to the work of the Association. It is one of mine and the Association's strengths in ensuring that ABS plays its role as an honest broker, with empathy and integrity, between the public and private sector agencies.

Having some degree of EQ, aptitude, hospitality, selflessness and passion is paramount to ensure that not only do the many projects we undertake get completed, but in a manner where everyone has fun while doing so.

A Gift for My Calling

Looking back, I realised that my interest in hosting others was already apparent from my younger days. My parents hailed from China and I grew up in a shophouse in Chinatown in the 50s. We lived upstairs while my father's office (his company was a remittance shop that also processed and distributed sugar) was housed downstairs. My parents took it upon themselves to open up the shophouse to be a 'port of call' of sorts for immigrants who had newly arrived from their hometown in Swatow, China.

The immigrants had their meals with us and slept downstairs on foldable canvas beds. My father would help them with remitting money and letters home and sourcing for employment as they adjusted to a foreign land. In order to feed everyone — up to 20 immigrants could be temporarily staying with us at any one time — we also employed an experienced restaurant chef to whip up the meals.

In between mealtimes, I noticed that the chef would be free in the afternoons. I jumped on the opportunity to get him to cook and prepare some snacks for my school mates from Raffles Institution and later for friends as well from university. These friends would get frequent invitations to tea parties in my home, and all of them were suitably impressed at being able to enjoy restaurant-quality food. For me, serving friends, and seeing them enjoying themselves, has always given me much pleasure.

The seeds of hospitality were planted then. From young, I was the one organising supper for my father's group of friends who played badminton at our home on Friday nights. I loved to do it, and would try to remember the likes and dislikes of each of his friends, and serve them accordingly. After I got married, I would also organise dinners for my husband's colleagues and friends at our home on weekends when I would cook up a storm.

Thus, it was no surprise that I wanted to go to the University of Hawaii for post-graduate studies in hospitality. However, I happened to meet my boyfriend then — now my late husband — and he had to also give up his Stanford University scholarship to complete National Service first, so we both remained in Singapore.

Though I did not manage to pursue hospitality academically, who knew that I would exercise these skills and get on-the-job training in this area when I joined ABS about a decade later?

I knew then that my gift of hospitality was nurtured in me since childhood for a reason and a purpose. It was to prepare me to be effective in my work at ABS, as we are often the diplomatic middleman who tries to help the different parties involved to reach a consensus and get things done. Of course, when I first joined ABS, I was not aware that this gift of mine would be crucial in the work that I would be doing.

Indeed, God's plans for us are always good, albeit mysterious at times.

With ABS walking the talk in championing good hospitality, we also encouraged the financial industry to improve their service standards by recognising the efforts of financial sector officers who delivered quality service. In 2007, ABS began conducting annual Excellent Service Award (EXSA), which is supported by SPRING Singapore.

Since then, ABS has honoured tens of thousands of award winners from banks and financial institutions, who receive gold, silver or star commendations based on criteria such as service attitude, communication skills including body language and the way they handled difficult situations.

When we serve others well, the level of intimacy we share with others increases. They will be more motivated to go beyond the usual rules of engagement to connect with and support you. Our Christian beliefs also influence how we host and treat others; the service is genuine and humble, and others are treated as more important than ourselves.

Chapter 15

The Awe of God

Li Bai, the Cantonese restaurant at Sheraton Towers, is named after the famous Chinese poet as it serves up fine Cantonese cuisine inspired by the poet's classical works. Its good food and comfortable seating make it a place conducive to work dinners.

While working on the draft of "ABS Guidelines on Sustainable Financing" for the banking industry in 2015, I realised that I needed a briefing on the subject from a friend of mine, Mr Peter Heng. He was then heading up the communications and sustainability department of a large oil palm company in Indonesia. At that time, the Southeast Asian region was also facing one of its worst haze and pollution crises ever.

As sustainable financing was a relatively new field then, I knew Peter was the right person for me to go to for advice as he had the relevant knowledge. Thus, I made an appointment to meet him for dinner after work at Li Bai, which was close to where we lived.

At the restaurant, I ordered some titbits to snack on while my colleague and I waited for Peter to arrive. Half an hour passed and there was still no sign of him, so I called him to ask after his whereabouts. It turned out that he had mixed up the date of our appointment and he was already in the midst of another engagement.

I was upset with his 'no show'. An internal debate raged within me. If we stayed on to have dinner, do I or does ABS foot the bill? I was irritated as, on the one hand, we had already ordered some food and it was not proper to leave as the crowded restaurant would lose a dinner seating. On the other hand, I would not have dined there if not for the pre-arranged work meeting.

Just as I was sitting there rationalising it all out, my younger son, Tze Ru, suddenly called me and asked me where I was. I ranted to him about my plight at being stuck in that restaurant and having to eat there just because my guest had pencilled in our appointment date wrongly.

Not knowing about the dilemma that I was struggling with, Tze Ru suddenly exclaimed over the phone: "Mum, you have to pay for the dinner, not the office!"

I was surprised and amused that the answer I was seeking for was delivered to me through my son.

In the past, I had witnessed how Christians, in moments of "weakness of the flesh", fell prey to temptation and give in to misconduct, bringing shame and dishonour not only to themselves and their family members, but also to God.

I have learnt that in order to guard myself against such potential misconduct, I cannot trust myself nor my heart, which the Word says is "more deceitful than all else and desperately sick". Only God knows my true motives. I constantly ask Him to search my heart and let me know if there are any unrighteous and evil ways in me that I may not be aware of. I need Him to bring them to my attention for repentance as I do not want to be caught doing the wrong thing, even if it is done inadvertently.

"And if I can't hear Your gentle warning," I told Him, "please give me a big kick to get my attention."

He showed up that day via my son's explicit instruction to remind me to do what is right.

After getting off the phone, I told my colleague what Tze Ru said and we proceeded to have a delightful dinner, which I gladly paid for.

I am so grateful to the Lord for keeping me on the straight and narrow path of His righteousness. I thank Him for giving me a yielded heart and submissive spirit. God truly honours the desire of my heart to 'never cross the line' in ethical or grey areas of the conscience by showing me the way to go in righteousness.

The Fear of the Lord

We often hear that having the fear of the Lord is the beginning of wisdom (Proverbs 9:10), but what does it mean to fear God? Proverbs 8:13 tells us that to fear the Lord is to hate evil, such as pride, arrogance, bad behaviour and perverse speech.

For me, this "fear of God" means having a heightened respect and an acknowledgement of Him in my life. He has given us the

Word for us to obey in order to avoid wrongdoing and evil, and to do rightly and act justly. As a Christian, I have become so concerned that my conduct may dishonour God that I am known for using this constant refrain in Teochew: "*Buay sai sia sway God*" (I must not bring disgrace upon God). I grew to love His discipline and admonishment, knowing that they are always done for my own good in building my character.

Generally, I know there is but a thin line between appreciation and bribery, or between respect and fawning. In ABS' role as the honest broker and middleman between regulators and banks, as well as between the private and public sector entities, I need to take extra caution in keeping an arm's length from all parties, even though we have good relationships with each other. This is so that ABS would not only be accepted by the banking industry as its voice and representative, but also be trusted and respected by the regulator, MAS and the government officers with whom it seeks to work closely.

Though there may be work partners who are my decades-long friends sitting in on official work meetings, we make sure that a certain decorum is upheld and that we do not bring our friendships into the meeting. Informal banter is fine, but when it comes to work matters, we cannot behave too casually with each other lest any professionalism is compromised.

When it comes to putting up papers or having official meetings, proposals are always supported by facts and figures; there is no such thing as "you scratch my back, I scratch yours". That also means that even though ABS is often a supporter of the policies and initiatives that MAS develops and rolls out, it also speaks up for the good of the industry should there be a need to. For instance, ABS also considers the business and practical aspects of proposals to ensure that Singapore remains competitive vis-à-vis other financial centres.

Thus, although ABS often works hand-in-hand with MAS, it is also an independent entity that is able to hold its own views in championing the needs and concerns of the sector.

In 2009 following the Global Financial Crisis, for example, MAS issued a consultation paper proposing to enhance the regulatory framework governing the sale and marketing of unlisted investment products.

In its feedback to MAS, ABS endorsed the well-meaning principles of the paper but took issue with one of the proposals to introduce a civil penalty regime. Introducing such a regime could make Singapore uncompetitive as a financial centre and the move would be costly, increase the risks to financial institutions and reduce choices and returns for investors.

The ABS Chairman and Council decided to push back against MAS' proposal for such a scheme. With the assistance of some member banks which had operations in the United Kingdom, Australia and Hong Kong, ABS sought the inputs of lawyers who had international experience in this area to put forth some alternative proposals to MAS instead.

Later that year, MAS informed ABS that it would not be proceeding with the proposed civil penalty regime. In this instance, we had to do what was necessary, and fortunately there was a good outcome.

Tales of Caution

One way that I keep myself in check is by taking special notice of articles in the newspaper which feature senior government officials or corporate leaders who were tempted by indiscretions and later charged for corruption, bribery, misappropriation of funds or abuse of power. They are grim reminders to me that temptations abound in the corporate world. These temptations usually revolve around three key areas of vulnerabilities: power and pride, money and greed, as well as relationship and abuse.

I would pray for these fallen leaders, without being critical or judgemental, and also ask the Lord to keep my "hands clean and heart pure" for His name's sake, by giving me the grace to keep from succumbing to temptations.

I don't trust myself in how I may react or behave in difficult situations, since even the Scripture describes how Peter, a close confidant and disciple of Jesus, failed and fell into temptation himself. He was so confident that he would never deny Jesus in the face of persecution, and yet on the eve of His crucifixion, Peter denied Jesus three times out of the fear of Man.

I vividly recall the time when an attractive woman — a representative from a foreign bank — gave me some practical advice in navigating temptations at the workplace. This was in the 70s when Singapore was opening her doors to foreign banks in her bid to become an international financial centre. I was working at MAS then and was involved in the licensing of banks. During the processing of the application for her bank, we had many meetings.

During one of our mealtime conversations, she noted that it was not uncommon for women in the banking industry to receive propositions from bankers. Some of these men travelled regularly and were often away from their homes and families. Whether from a state of loneliness or when reeling from the 'high' of alcohol, some of them would compliment us women freely and copiously. The onus then, she warned me, was on us to be careful so that we do not have 'stars in our eyes' and get carried away by their attention. Otherwise, the consequences on our conscience, marriage and families could be dire. Over the years, I bore her advice in mind, took the necessary caution and trusted God to deliver me from all temptations.

A Higher Standard of Governance

Once, when ABS had a change of auditors, the new auditor made a teasing remark when he came in: "I hope I don't find a Madoff here!" Bernie Madoff was infamously known for operating history's largest Ponzi scheme that defrauded investors around the world for decades.

I told him confidently that I live and work for an "audience of One" and that the governance that I live by is higher than what any human being can set with rules and guidelines. His standard is so high that if any man should so much as look lustfully at a woman — even without touching her — it would be deemed as adultery!

I live in the fear of the Lord, knowing that He knows everything. Nothing — not even our fleeting sinful thoughts — can be hidden from Him.

I recognise that it is easy for a successful leader to abuse his or her position since others around them tend to defer to them. Thus, I constantly ask the Lord to keep me in check so that I would not cross any lines.

I would also tell the accounts division to keep strictly to accounting principles, notwithstanding what I say or tell them to do. I cautioned them not to say, whether out of fear or deference to me: "… but Mrs Ong told me to do it." If they do not feel comfortable with any actions or instructions, they should not hesitate to speak up.

Though I often take responsibility for everything, including the errors made by my team, I would remind the accounts people that they would still need to exercise their own professional responsibility to call out any discrepancies or misdemeanours.

At ABS, expenses are subjected to the year's budget and they have to be approved by the Council, tracked by the accounts division and signed off by dual signatories, such as myself and the Chairman bank's representative.

It is my heartfelt desire to not only finish well in the marathon of life but also in the light of eternity. Therefore, I am conscious of the need to be honest, truthful and sincere in all my dealings with people. After becoming a Christian, I react differently when my mistakes are pointed out by others. Instead of feeling criticised or rejected, I do not take it as personally as I used to, but see it as, perhaps, a check from the Lord to reconsider my behaviour and motives.

I would pray about it and read His Word while thinking about the issue at hand. If I am in the wrong, I know I need to quickly humble myself and apologise. The point of it all is to get myself right with God. I have learnt to not be affected by how the other party responds to my apology, as long as my conscience is clear in the sight of God.

I find that it always helps to speak the truth plainly, instead of fudging matters. If I have made an error or oversight, I would rather admit it instead of hiding it out of fear of embarrassment, chastisement or repercussion. The Bible in Ephesians 5:11 reminds us to take "no part in the worthless deeds of evil and darkness; instead, expose them". Only then would I find peace within me, with my conscience clear.

In 2022, we were having a Dr Goh Keng Swee Scholarship Fund board meeting when the topic of raising additional funds to sustain the scholarship was discussed. Then, a board member — Mr Piyush Gupta — turned to me and asked why the funds had not yet been raised, since we had talked about it the year before and I was asked to follow up on it.

Instead of trying to defend myself or cover things up, I decided to be honest with him and the board members. I told them I took my foot off the accelerator for this project as I was disappointed when I found out the year before that the donors who funded this would not receive double tax deduction as we were not an Institution of a Public Character. That made it harder for me to convince the banks to donate and support this project. After explaining myself, I reassured them that I would look into the matter and the board accepted it. In the end, an additional $5 million was raised for the scholarship fund which would support students from the Asia-Pacific region to do their undergraduate studies in Singapore.

Even as I put in place good personal accountability and corporate governance practices for ABS, the Association also played a key role in safeguarding the confidential information of customers in the larger sector.

Evolving Threats

It was December 2013, and a large foreign bank had hastily called a press conference on a Thursday night. The bank had been notified by the Singapore Police that 647 of its private bank clients' monthly bank statements for February that year had been stolen. The theft did not occur through the bank's IT and data security systems, but from a third-party service provider — a printing company. The bank statements had contained detailed, highly confidential information such as the clients' address and the amount of funds they held with the bank.

MAS came down hard on the bank. It didn't matter that the printing job was outsourced; they were still held responsible. While no unauthorised transactions were made with the stolen information, MAS said the incident underscored "the need for heightened vigilance in financial institutions, including close management of risks pertaining to service providers".

Over at ABS, there was a realisation that a standardised audit process was needed to prevent future mishaps of a similar nature. This kickstarted a massive exercise to get all the banks' outsourced service providers (OSPs) to comply with MAS' technology risk requirements.

ABS had to request from all the banks their lists of OSPs (we also had to convince the banks and the OSPs of the commercial benefit of doing so) and get all the OSPs to be audited before the banks could engage them for their services.

It was a huge undertaking. Many rounds of meetings were conducted with the different stakeholders to standardise the audit methodology. Following that, ABS established the Guidelines on Control Objectives and Procedures for the OSPs, which form the baseline controls for OSPs that intend to service financial institutions. We named it the Outsourced Service Provider's Audit Report, or OSPAR for short. Finally, after two years, we managed to get the banking industry and the OSPs to understand, accept and adopt OSPAR.

OSPAR would go on to be adopted by other commercial sectors, as it ensured a high level of compliance by the OSPs. We had set a sterling standard and others also rode on it.

Good governance is important because it brings with it many benefits. It reduces risks, enables faster and safer growth, as well as improves the reputation and trust levels within and without the organisation. All these would help to ensure ABS' longevity in the long run.

Over the years, ABS has been running a tight ship in keeping its operational costs low. Yet fortuitously, with the additional annual dividends, its reserves have been growing steadily year on year to more than $11 million to date, making ABS a productive and fruitful organisation. This can only be achieved by applying certain principles of good governance, such as accountability and transparency.

My journey to attaining these favourable outcomes was not the result of knowing what good governance practices to put in place. More often than not, I was pretty unsure about all these processes and practices. In murky situations when I was uncertain about what to do, the Holy Spirit guided me.

By His grace, as I strived to be more like Christ and tried to do the right thing according to His Word, I found myself moving in the right direction.

Chapter 16

The Digital Dinosaur Becomes Ms AI

From 2011 onwards, the world saw the Fourth Industrial Revolution with the digitalisation of manufacturing. Dubbed Industry 4.0, it came after the first, second and third industrial revolution of mechanisation through water and steam power, then mass production through electricity and eventually, the adoption of computers and automation. Now, smart and autonomous systems are fuelled by data and machine learning, and addressed via the Internet of Things.

Such technical terms initially seemed Greek to me. I was intimidated by my lack of knowledge and expertise in these areas. Once again, I had a strong sense of unease and foreboding when Prime Minister Lee Hsien Loong outlined plans to turn Singapore into the world's first Smart Nation in 2014.

It felt like déjà vu as I harboured a similar dread in 1999 when I felt inadequate to lead ABS into the dot-com era. I wanted to resign then but did not do so in the end.

This time, my reservations about leading the organisation during a time of heightened digitalisation and communication between smart machines had not yet led me to the point of wanting to quit my job, but I had major concerns about my capability, or lack thereof.

People around me know that I often refer to myself as the 'Queen of Analogue' or 'The Digital Dinosaur'. I am slow in picking up digital skills and lack the intuitiveness in using devices and gadgets as I do not have an interest in them. Rather, I am a tactile person who loves the feel of writing on paper and reading physical printouts or books. What thrills me the most is not receiving an iPad, but heading to a stationery shop to stock up on all the pens and notebooks that I usually use.

It was with such worries and a heavy heart that I stepped into church one Sunday in 2014. As the church choir sang the song "Oceans" by Hillsong United, I felt the Lord speaking to me and singing over me.

The lyrics of the song went:

You call me out upon the waters
The great unknown where feet may fail
And there I find You in the mystery
In oceans deep my faith will stand

And I will call upon Your Name
And keep my eyes above the waves
When oceans rise
My soul will rest in Your embrace
For I am Yours and You are mine

Your grace abounds in deepest waters
Your sovereign hand will be my guide
Where feet may fail and fear surrounds me
You've never failed and You won't start now

I began weeping. It was the rhema word that I needed: I felt God was speaking directly to me through the lyrics of the song. He knew my fears about venturing, once again, into the deep, uncharted waters of digital projects and smart nation initiatives. He used the song to calm me down and speak into the issues that were troubling me.

It was more than an emotional encouragement; it was a divine reassurance that He had always been there for me and would continue to be there for me even as I meet future challenges.

Soon after, the MAS appointed Mr Sopnendu Mohanty, formerly from Citibank, as its new Chief Fintech Officer. I was introduced to him and we hit it off from the get-go. He was young, light-hearted and energetic, especially when talking about technology. Whenever he came by my office, he would share his digital knowledge and ideas with me, and we would also discuss other life issues over cups of *teh tarik*.

He knew that ABS would be the most relevant and appropriate body to move fintech ideas among the banks. Although he also knew of my limited knowledge in fintech, it did not deter him as he saw me as a feisty woman passionate about my work, who had a 'template' to be able to bring the banks together to work effectively on projects. We established a good rapport with each other.

At the same time, with digital industry projects starting to emerge on the horizon, the ABS Banking Technology unit was established in 2018. It comprises former bankers with domain knowledge in technology. Starting with an initial team of five, the unit has more than doubled to 12 as the Association took on more and more digitalisation initiatives over the past few years.

Singapore Fintech Festival

One day in 2015, Sopnendu floated the idea of having a Singapore Fintech Festival (SFF) for five days at the Singapore Expo. Mr Roy Teo, then Director of the Fintech and Innovation Group at the MAS, asked me and Shimah if ABS would help to organise it. Excitement overtook us as it was a new thing, unlike the routine ABS events that we usually organise.

The topic was also a relevant one for the future. Fintech had so much potential and it could create greater value for the banks if both spheres were connected.

We talked about it and realised that we would make a good team. On the one hand, I may have been a 'digital dinosaur' but my forte was in mobilising the banks and organising events.

On the other hand, Sopnendu, Roy and the MAS team had the technical knowledge and contacts to curate the Fintech Festival programme. But they needed help with garnering support from the banks and with pulling off the event. Back then, Singapore's banks were chilly towards fintech. Doubts lingered over whether such a collaboration could work, or if the fintech firms would come in and 'steal their lunch' by providing services that usurp the functions of financial institutions.

Sopnendu estimated that the inaugural festival would accommodate about 1,000 participants. I went back to Shimah to check if we had the capacity to execute the logistics for an event of this size. She replied in the affirmative, and I also felt the conviction in my heart that this would be the right thing to do for the industry, given that fintech would likely be the order of the day soon.

However, when the event was tabled at the ABS Council meeting for approval, it received a lukewarm reception as fintech was still in its infancy and there was apprehension as to how the banks would work with fintech companies. After we debated over the need for the fintech event, the Council did not make a concluding decision to either support or decline it. It was God's wisdom that guided me to leave the matter as it was, without pushing the Council for a definitive decision on the project. As long as they did not outrightly reject it, I was still left with room to continue supporting the festival by helping Sopnendu to organise it.

I discerned that organising such a fintech festival was the right thing to do. Apart from having such a conviction, I also felt the peace in my heart to do it. Moreover, it surprisingly did not feel like work; it was something new and so it actually felt fun! Perhaps it was my pioneering spirit coming into play. I derive immense satisfaction from creating and developing new things, especially if it taps on my strength and giftings.

ABS went ahead to take up the challenge of organising the first Singapore Fintech Festival, in partnership with MAS, that took place in 2016.

Then there were five staff in the ABS events team, two of whom were recent hires. It was all hands on deck. We had to source for good vendors and suppliers, and look into organising not only the main event at the Singapore Expo but also the fringe events to be held at hotels.

We also needed to raise money for the event. Sopnendu and his MAS team sought out the main sponsors.

Yet our team at ABS was ready to venture out of our comfort zone and learn new things in event organisation to create a new conference experience for the participants.

In order to create a dynamic and futuristic atmosphere for a side event, we researched LED walls and brought them in as backdrops. We also searched out different hip and cool-looking sofas and chairs to be used for panel discussions.

Avoiding the usual catered food, we secured live stations to serve food à la minute — burgers and freshly cooked fries from a food truck and steaming hot paella from a giant wok — so as to inject an added element of fun into the event.

Shifting Goalposts

As the months of preparation went along, Sopnendu and Roy would come by our office periodically to discuss the progress of the project. Initially, Sopnendu suggested increasing the number of participants of the event from 1,000 to 2,000. We agreed as we saw that he had a good programme curated with prominent thought leaders, hence meriting a larger crowd. Subsequently, he increased the number of participants to 4,000, and then to 6,000.

At that time, we were so enthusiastic about the event that we kept accepting the new numbers. We were excited about hosting more people and the Christians in the ABS team prayed for the Lord's favour to help us with the growing numbers. There was unity between ABS and MAS in our vision for this project.

When Sopnendu turned up one day and suggested raising the number of participants further to 8,000, we laughed as the event was really getting bigger and bigger. We had to stop him from further increasing the number as we feared that we might not be able to cope with the registration and collaterals. He reluctantly agreed.

However, when we made the announcement on social media that registration for the first Singapore Fintech Festival would be closed at 8,000 signups, the number of registrants actually jumped overnight to 10,000! We could not turn them away. By the opening day of the event, the number shot up by another few thousands through walk-ins, to a total of almost 13,000.

By then, my great concern was blowing the budget that MAS and ABS had raised for this event. I knew I was taking a risk in deciding to go ahead with organising the event without having the explicit consent of the ABS Council. It meant that if there was any deficit, I would not be able to recover it from the Association, so I was mentally prepared to fork out the balance from my own pocket. I also tapped into my networks and called up the banks and service providers to persuade them to contribute to the event as well — something I'm grateful they did.

I prayed daily for the event to at least break even in terms of finances.

Even as we worked hard at organising the logistics for this mega event, we could not have pulled it off if we did not have the favour and provision of God.

As the numbers went up, we needed more welcome bags to be given to each participant at the conference. It was the first time we had engaged this supplier— a young man — and we were worried about whether he would be able to supply additional orders of the bags at such short notice. It turned out that he was so committed to making sure that all the stocks would arrive in Singapore on time that he flew over to China to personally oversee the logistical arrangements.

Together with Roy, we spotted a few mistakes in the official programme brochure at the last minute, so we only managed to finalise the programme for print at 2am on Friday, the last day before the festival weekend. When we entered the parking lot of the building at Loyang where the printing company, MediaLink, was located, we saw a solitary car in the lot that belonged to its boss. He had been waiting to get the final copy of the programme to commence printing. His team also returned on a Saturday morning to make sure sufficient copies were printed, at no extra cost for the overtime hours.

The boss and his team at the printing company were willing to go the extra mile for us because we had a longstanding relationship with them. Over the years, we had cultivated good relationships with vendors, suppliers and hotels by being a prompt paymaster and being fair in our dealings with them, such as not short-changing them and not being restrained by the terms stipulated in the contracts.

God also provided us with the manpower needed to pack the thousands of welcome bags that were to be filled with gifts from the sponsors. Although there were only five of us in the events team, we managed to rope in our friends and families to pitch in. All together 20 of us did the job — factory line style — in one room, and we surprisingly completed all the packing within a day!

We managed to get all the extra help we needed by asking the children of our staff as well as friends to help with registration and ushering at the fringe events. Even the daughter of our admin officer went up on stage during the award night at Universal Studios to help with the award presentation ceremony.

Shimah also recounted to me how God gave her the idea to set up an official SFF merchandise booth that sold items — T-shirts, tote bags or mouse pads — with the official SFF logo. Since then, ABS has retained the franchise to continue selling SFF merchandise at all subsequent SFF annual events. Over the years, the merchandise has proven to be especially popular with overseas delegates. The limited-edition merchandise helped to build up the SFF branding and defray some costs.

On 14 November 2016, about 13,000 participants streamed through the doors of the sprawling Singapore Expo. The five-day event, featuring 73 exhibitors and the Global Fintech Hackcelerator, was an impressive debut. Plaudits came from all quarters, including overseas visitors such as those from the fast-emerging fintech hub, Dublin.

"It was the first attempt at a hugely ambitious project and organisers should be applauded for their daring," read Dublin's popular tech website Irish Tech News. "It was a smoothly run production with high-profile speakers and top-notch commentary. The Singapore Fintech Festival has now firmly established itself as a global leader in this industry."

After the event, when it was time to work out the cost of the event for ABS, I continued to pray for at least a break even in the numbers. It was then that Shimah asked me a question: "Mrs Ong, how many commas are there in a million?" She was puzzled as there seemed to be more figures after the commas than she had expected.

She handed me the accounts. I saw that the festival had garnered us $1.45 million. A huge wave of relief washed over me. I am thankful that the event went very well for Singapore and MAS.

Today, the SFF has become the fintech industry's largest event and its dates have been pencilled into the calendars of the likes of Microsoft co-founder Bill Gates, Google CEO Sundar Pichai, Prime Minister of India Narendra Modi and President of the European Central Bank Christine Lagarde, among a growing alumni list of renowned SFF speakers.

In subsequent years, ABS remained a partner of the SFF but its logistics was taken over by a specialised events management company. The burgeoning turnout would have been too much for ABS to handle.

Last year, for instance, SFF 2022 — the seventh edition of the SFF — attracted more than 62,000 participants from over 115 countries.

In hindsight, we would not have said "yes" to organising and co-spearheading the first festival in 2016 if we had known that the turnout would be about 13,000 participants. We had only agreed to the initial estimation of 1,000 and, with only five of us at ABS, we would not have thought that we could handle it.

Sometimes, this is how God works. He does not show us the grand goal or endpoint as we may become too intimidated or distracted by it. All we did was to say a few "yes"es along the way as the target numbers expanded. As we did our best, He also grew our capacity and supplied us with His favour and provision every step of the way.

When I am Weak, Then I am Strong

At the latest run of the SFF in 2022, some of the hot topics included artificial intelligence (AI), sustainable finance and stablecoins development.

In my welcome address at the 2022 SFF Global FinTech Award Night held at Resorts World Sentosa, I remarked to the audience how, even with the advent of the new era of digitalisation, I was a digital dinosaur and queen of analogue. I do not have much understanding of fintech or AI, but thanks to my parents, "Ai" is my middle name. They laughed.

Following the adoption of fintech initiatives by the industry, ABS also went on to support and undertake several digital projects such as e-payment system eGiro, PayNow and the Trade Finance Registry.

It was back in June 2015 when MAS' Managing Director Mr Ravi

Menon first shared Singapore's aspiration to be a Smart Financial Centre. "A Smart Nation needs a Smart Financial Centre," he said, alluding to the launch of Singapore's Smart Nation vision by Prime Minister Lee Hsien Loong just eight months before. Ravi is the longest serving Managing Director at MAS (2011 to present). He was named the Asia Pacific Central Banker of the Year in 2018 by The Banker. MAS was named Central Bank of the year in 2019 by Central Banking.

"The financial sector is well placed to play a leading role given that financial services offer fertile ground for innovation and the application of technology. MAS will partner the industry to work towards the vision of a Smart Financial Centre, where innovation is pervasive and technology is used widely to increase efficiency, create new opportunities, manage risks better and improve people's lives."

MAS said it would seek to achieve this vision together with the industry through two broad thrusts. Firstly, it would be done through having a regulatory approach that is conducive to innovation while fostering safety and security. Secondly, there would be development initiatives to create a vibrant ecosystem for innovation as well as to adopt new technologies.

The vision was backed by a $225 million Financial Sector Technology and Innovation scheme to provide funding for the setup of innovation centres and catalyse the development of innovative solutions by financial institutions, as well as to support the building of industry-wide technology infrastructure required for the delivery of new and integrated services.

A year later at the inaugural Singapore Fintech Festival, Ravi also noted: "To be sure, many of these technologies are disruptive to existing jobs and existing business models. But if we do not disrupt ourselves in a manner we choose, somebody else will, in a manner we will not like."

Disruption certainly came a-knocking that season, both for ABS and myself.

Of all people, why would such a dinosaur and analogue queen suddenly be thrust into the fast-paced digital world of fintech and AI to play a role in it? It's ironic but that is how God works. He chooses "the foolish things of the world to shame the wise and the weak things of the world to shame the strong" (1 Corinthians 1:27), so that His "power is made perfect in weakness" (2 Corinthians 12:9).

It is only when I am weak that I find myself totally dependent on God, trusting Him to work things out on my behalf. This is key so that, if there are any successes or breakthroughs, especially in the areas of my weaknesses, all credit goes to Him and none to myself.

Disruption — or rather, the Lord's interruption — brought reassurance of His unchanging care for me. Indeed, as the lyrics of the song "Oceans" describes it, God has seen me through the deepest of waters when I felt totally out of my depth. I believe His faithfulness and guidance will continue to see me through other changing seasons in ABS and in my life, technological or otherwise.

I first met Ai Boon in 1983 when she chaired a meeting on the rollout of GIRO between the banks and BCS, which was to operate the system. I was then 23 and was working for BCS in charge of the Project Office. I was immediately struck by how Ai Boon was able to galvanise everyone towards common goals.

As it turned out over the next 38 years until I retired in 2021, I would go on to work closely with her as she consistently engaged the relevant parties with clarity of mission and direction on many industry projects. These included SHIFT (System for Handling Interbank Funds Transfers), Same-Day Cheque Clearing, the Scripless Government Securities system, ECS (Electronic Clearing System), eGIRO, CTS (Cheque Truncation System), MEPS+ (MAS Electronic Payments System), FAST (Fast and Secure Transfers) and PayNow.

In all our time working together, I've known Ai Boon to have this unflinching "can do" spirit and a positive mindset. This book floods back memories of how oftentimes she was able to induce support from key stakeholders and the industry to turn things around when the chips were down and the challenges appeared insurmountable.

Jimmy Quek
Former MD,
Banking Computer Services

Part 5

A New Season

Chapter 17

A Change in Leadership Style

At the Singapore FinTech Festival 2022 Award night held at Resorts World Sentosa, MAS' Managing Director Mr Ravi Menon took the stage to give his opening remarks.

I sat in my seat and listened diffidently as Ravi publicly thanked and affirmed me.

"Much of what we have achieved in Singapore would not have been possible if not for the close collaboration between the MAS and The Association of Banks in Singapore. And Ai Boon, as you know, is the pillar of strength at ABS who has galvanised, mobilised and made many things happen," he said. "So, don't let her fool you with her remarks about being Miss Analogue. She is actually Ms AI, in disguise."

Over the years, I have let both criticism and compliments roll off me like water off a duck's back. As a prophet previously mentioned, it was as if I wore a coat made of Teflon where remarks from others, whether positive or negative, do not stick to me. That is because I have learnt to be secure in who I am and who God made me to be, so I need not be overly affected by external praise or disapproval.

Yet that night, I felt a bit self-conscious, and even shy, at the commendation given. Not wanting to draw much attention, I kept mostly to myself and my table at the ballroom though I would usually be found mingling with the other guests.

I dug deep and reflected. Why was I feeling and behaving this way? I was 76 going on to 77 years old by then, and having lived and worked through so many decades, surely I ought to have already attained a certain level of confidence by now?

I thought of the time when I once commented, during a conversation with DBS CEO Mr Piyush Gupta, that I was not up to the standard in question. He turned to me and surprised me with his reply, saying: "Ai Boon, come on, don't underestimate yourself. You are one of the few people I have worked with who moves the needle."

Caught off-guard with such compliments, I was left speechless.

The closer we get to the end, I realised, the more we find ourselves at the beginning. I am slowly becoming aware of how my experiences in my teenage years continues to affect how I view myself, even now.

The seeds of low self-esteem had been planted in my life more than six decades ago when I began believing in the lie that I was stupid.

I was enrolled in the pure science stream at Crescent Girls' School after completing primary school at Fairfield Methodist Girls' School. It was the wrong discipline for me as I was not cut out for subjects such as maths and science. In those four years, I failed those subjects very badly. I began internalising ungodly beliefs that I could not study or do well in anything, and that I was not smart.

My parents were supportive and did not pressure me at all. They encouraged me to opt for a more practical course to train as a beautician and hairdresser if I felt that academics was not my strong suit. Yet those years of failure also made me resilient. I did not give up and sat for the 'O' levels exams but performed poorly.

When my father later asked if I wanted a second chance at studying again, I agreed. He got me a place in Singapore Chinese Girls' School. This time, I chose the humanities track and, surprisingly, I blossomed. Within one year, I scored distinctions in subjects such as history, geography and literature, and I had an 'O' level score that was good enough to get me admitted into Raffles Institution.

It turned out that I was not stupid after all, but had failed earlier because I was a round peg forced into a square hole. However, unknown to me, those beliefs that I had internalised about myself had gone so deep into my psyche that they remained there for decades. At times, they bubble up to the surface, leaving me feeling inadequate and fearful.

Later on, I would have a revelation that all these things that had happened in the past could have been "of the Lord", in order to keep me humble in life and dependent on Him. This insight came when I was reading about the life of Samson and came across the verses in Judges 14:4: "His parents did not know that this was from the Lord, who was seeking an occasion to confront the Philistines; for at that time they were ruling over Israel."

Samson was attracted to a beautiful Philistine girl and had asked his parents to get her for him as his wife. The parents chastised him for not choosing one from among their own tribe as it was the ordinance of God for them not to marry outside their tribe. Yet they did not know it was God who had orchestrated such a situation to bring about His purposes for His people. He knows the end from the beginning and truly His ways and thoughts are higher than our ways and thoughts.

A Change in Leadership Style

Despite my hang-ups, God still groomed me as a leader in phases, in His way and in His time. The first phase of 20 years saw me being guided by eight Singaporean banking stalwarts as Chairmen even as I learnt how to lead ABS. The second phase saw me rising up in greater measure to work more independently and to guide ABS' Chairmen, many of whom were foreigners, as the sector liberalised. Nearly another two decades later, in 2019, I did not expect to be shifted into yet another phase of leadership.

My daughter-in-law, Jing Yin, had been an Ear, Nose & Throat (ENT) Consultant at Khoo Teck Puat Hospital and went on to hone her expertise in the field of laryngology (voice and swallowing disorders). In 2019, she was awarded funding to head to Sydney, Australia, for further training in the field.

She had planned to bring her two young children — three-year-old Megan and one-year-old Matthew — along with her while her husband Tze Ru remained in Singapore to work. Though she would be engaging a housekeeper in Sydney to help out, I was worried about whether she would be able to cope with juggling solo parenting and working at the same time.

I thought hard about the matter and prayed for favour from the then ABS Chairmen to allow me to work out of Sydney for a year, so that I could help keep an eye on my two grandchildren. I thank God that the Chairman then — Mr Piyush Gupta from DBS, and the incoming one, Mr Samuel Tsien from OCBC — gave their support for me to work remotely. I assured them that it would be business as usual and that my presence would not be missed as I would still fly to and fro whenever necessary to attend important meetings.

In March 2019, I left for Sydney and was scheduled to return the following year. Fortuitously, a new batch of experienced and mature managers in their 50s and 60s joined ABS in the year before I left. They had domain knowledge and experience with the type of projects that ABS usually undertakes.

By then I, too, had gained sufficient experience to be able to guide them by explaining the various protocols and procedures common to the Association. I could also anticipate problems early enough to give them timely advice before the issues occurred.

Thus, though I was away, I was able to issue instructions on the phone or via email, and feel confident enough to trust them to follow through on the projects. It helped that Shimah, who by then had taken on the function of ABS' Chief Operating Officer, could help hold the fort at ABS.

This season thrust me into a different phase of leadership. I had no choice but to let go and learn how to mentor and teach my staff from afar, while entrusting them with the actual execution of the tasks.

In the past, I had younger and less experienced staff. Whenever there were any hiccups, I would (due to my habitual impatience and penchant for micromanaging) take over the work and do it myself most of the time. Worse still, I often blamed or scolded them if I spotted any issues or mistakes.

The sudden need to work off-site forced me to shift gears and instead seek to empower my team by learning how to give good advice and instructions. Instead of trying to be a perfectionist by handholding them, I let go and depended on God to give me the discernment I needed to spot problems before they occurred.

My time away in Sydney therefore marked a watershed moment in the shift of my leadership style to one that involved more teaching, empowering and mentoring.

Looking back, I am amazed at His impeccable timing in sending me to Sydney at a time when ABS had just onboarded a team of senior executives whom I could trust to be guided from afar. The timing was also divine because by then, Shimah the COO had become well versed with the processes and protocols needed to assist them so that I was able to continue advising and directing remotely. When the COVID-19 pandemic took the world by storm the following year, we were well-prepared and adjusted well to the changes needed on the work front at ABS.

Having an experienced team to run the projects at ABS, and having a smooth transition even when COVID hit, were provisions of His grace at a time when I needed it the most.

Chapter 18

Levelling the Mountain

During our time in Sydney, my daughter-in-law, Jing Yin, began experiencing difficulty with her speech and found herself constantly being asked to repeat herself. It was puzzling as she used to speak as loudly as a canon and as fast as a machine gun.

She was eventually diagnosed with Motor Neurone Disease (MND), an uncommon condition that affects the nerves and muscles. It causes muscular atrophy that gets worse over time.

There is no cure for MND, but there are treatments to help reduce the impact it has on a person's daily life. Some people live with the condition for many years but MND can significantly shorten life expectancy.

From then on, she struggled to speak and be understood. It was ironic that she was afflicted in the very area that she specialised in.

She had to cut short her one-year training stint in Sydney and we returned to Singapore after only eight months there.

Instead of returning to my own home, I was invited by my younger son Tze Ru and Jing Yin to move in straightaway with their family. They would need all the help they could get with caregiving for Jing Yin and with parenting their two children.

A day after the doctor in Sydney diagnosed Jing Yin with the disease, Mr Daniel Sim, the eldest son of Pastor Dr CJ Sim, who had no prior knowledge of what we were going through then, sent me a verse to encourage me he said. Daniel pastors with his father at the Resurrection Life Ministries, a church in Brisbane. Pastor CJ Sim and his late wife, Sis Siew Hong, are good friends. I had been invited for a consecutive 10 years, prior to the COVID pandemic, to teach at the annual School of Ministry in Brisbane.

The verse shared by Daniel was from Zechariah 4:6–7 where the Lord said to Zerubbabel and the mountain that he was facing: "Not by might nor by power, but by my Spirit ... What are you, mighty mountain? Before Zerubbabel you will become level ground. Then he will bring out the capstone to shouts of 'Grace! Grace!'"

Great faith arose in me when I received the Holy Spirit-led rhema word from God. I believe that God will level the mountain and heal my daughter-in-law. The doctors might not be able to do anything about her condition nor her own body heal itself. Only the Holy Spirit can perform the miracle in His time.

However, I also believe that we need to be partners with God in the journey of healing and cooperate with His Word by standing on His promises. The great mountain mentioned in the Bible verse refers to the trials and problems that we face in life. In our trials, there could be certain aspects or 'mountains' in our lives that need to be dealt with and overcome before we see the bigger breakthrough. It is not by our own works but by the grace of God.

In my initial understanding of the verses, the great mountain for Jing Yin is the MND that she needs to overcome by allowing the Holy Spirit to take over as she trusts God with what she is going through. I stand in intercession as Zerubbabel did, believing in the grace of God for her.

Over the past three years, as I meditated further on the verses, the Holy Spirit revealed to me that there are three peaks on this great mountain. One would concern Jing Yin, the second her husband Tze Ru and the third, me.

As both Jing Yin and her husband are of "one flesh" through marriage, both of them need to come in alignment in faith and love as His Word says husband and wife are to be one in the Spirit. They can be so different in their thinking that there is a need for them to come together in spiritual unity.

It did not cross my mind then, even as I contended for her healing, that there was also a mountain peak for me to overcome as well when I moved in to live with them in this new season of my life.

Control and Offence

My mother, a 94-year-old widow, had lived with me for 10 years before she died in her sleep in 2019. After her demise, I had planned to renovate the apartment I was living in and continue to be the Queen of my house in my golden years since my children all had their own homes and families.

Little did I expect that all those plans would go out of the window. I thought that God was done teaching me about submission after I had learnt to submit — first to my husband, then to my bosses. Who knew that I would have to undergo further training in submission when I came under the authority of my son upon moving into their home?

When one is in close proximity with family, it is easy to see everyone's warts and all, and to rub each other the wrong way. I realised I had never been offended by anyone to the extent that I was while under their roof. There were three classic examples that showed me how offended I could get with my daughter-in-law, despite my love for her.

Once, my granddaughter Megan (then six years old) wanted to have some strawberries at 11am, an hour before we were due to have lunch. So, I cut a few strawberries and was about to pass them to her. I noticed that Jing Yin (who was largely unable to talk by then) kept mumbling under her breath for me not to give Megan any strawberries. I tried to explain to Jing Yin that it was a full hour before lunch and the strawberries would likely not affect Megan's appetite for lunch later.

She was probably frustrated at me arguing back because I immediately received a call from my son who was out of the house at that time.

"Mum, do not give Megan the strawberries," Tze Ru told me firmly over the phone.

It was just seven words, but that short instruction made me livid.

I went into my room and took up the issue with God. I ranted to Him about the reasons I wanted to give Megan strawberries: It was some time before lunch and strawberries, being acidic, ought to increase Megan's appetite for lunch instead of dulling it. After I was done explaining, God only had one line in response to my verbose complaining.

He said: "It is not about the strawberries; it is about control."

Upon hearing that, I could not help but burst out laughing.

It was true. The issue at stake was really about the wrestling of control over the children and who gets the final say in the house. I had forgotten that I was no longer 'in charge' of the household. I then told both my son and daughter-in-law what God had said to me and I apologised to them.

I needed to repent, give up the control that I was used to (as well as my rights and pride) and remind myself that I was there simply to love and serve them.

Yet another similar incident happened shortly after. I was about to rush off for an appointment in the evening when my grandson, Matthew (then four years old), told me that he was hungry. In the corner of the kitchen, I noticed there was a roast chicken that was covered by aluminium foil. So, I lifted the foil and began to slice the chicken to give some to him.

It was then I heard guttural sounds from the room. I headed in and asked Jing Yin what she wanted. She was annoyed and indicated to me that the chicken had to "rest" after roasting and could not be sliced too quickly. I explained to her that her son was hungry and I was in a rush, so I sliced the chicken to serve it to him. Anyway, the chicken seemed to have been sitting out there for some time.

My son heard us and came over, asking what the commotion was about. When I explained the matter, he promptly took the side of his wife and said: "Yes Mum, this is her chicken, not your chicken."

I was furious and stormed out of the house for my appointment immediately. That night, my heart was so distracted by the issue that I even missed a scheduled conference call.

When I spoke to God about it, He began to show me that I needed to ask for her permission before cutting the chicken. I may have been her mother-in-law, but I was wrong for taking things into my own hands, no matter how good my reasons were. It was indeed "her chicken and not my chicken".

The next morning, Jing Yin asked me to pray for her as she had choked twice during dinner the night before.

"Jing Yin, your choking has nothing to do with your medical condition," I told her.

"Are you angry with your mother-in-law for cutting up your chicken last night? I was so angry about the incident that I forgot to attend a scheduled conference call last night. I apologise for cutting your chicken before seeking your permission to do so. You also have to forgive your mother-in-law because, when you are angry, the muscles in your gullet freeze and cause the choking. You need to forgive everyone who has offended you. Healing comes with it."

There was a third time — again involving food — when God revealed to me the state of my own stubborn and wilful heart in wanting to do things my way. This time it was over the cooking of a piece of barramundi for dinner. My daughter-in-law had typed out on WhatsApp her recipe for me to follow when I cook the fish; it included steps on when to add butter, salt, garlic and white wine.

However, when I saw that the rest of the dinner dishes were Chinese and not Western cuisine, my mind went on auto-pilot mode and I decided to fry the fish with black sauce instead, so as to have it better complement the rest of the dishes. I had forgotten about her cooking instructions.

When she saw the dish, she was upset that I had ignored her instructions. Despite her physical handicap, she had painstakingly typed out the instructions for me. She was frustrated that her full instructions could not be executed because she could not move or speak. My son, who understood why I did what I did, went to console his wife. Then, he explained to me that this matter was not just about what was deemed to be the right thing to do, but understanding that, given Jing Yin's physical condition, it was a form of therapy for her to experiment and create a new dish for the children.

I realised my error and felt really bad about still needing to do things my way. I went to God and confessed that I had a callous heart that did not care enough for Jing Yin, but was glad that her husband understood where each of us was coming from. I was reminded of the verse in 2 Chronicles 25:2, where King Amaziah did "what was right in the sight of the Lord, yet not with a whole heart". Once again, I knew that I could be so right with all the reasons for why I did what I did, yet I could be so wrong with God. I am grateful that God was working on my deep-seated self-centredness; I needed to learn to consider others as more important than myself.

These conflicts came after I had prayed to God to help me be His instrument of peace and blessing in the family, instead of being viewed as a difficult mother and mother-in-law that they regret having around, especially given the already challenging situation at home with Jing Yin's physical condition.

Even in this new and advanced season of my life, it is so edifying to know that God still cares about teaching me how to relinquish dominating control both at work and at home. I am learning about submission all over again (this time with my son and daughter-in-law), and how to have an "un-offendable" heart. As the peace prayer often attributed to St Francis of Assisi goes, may it be that I "may not so much seek to be understood as to understand".

Reclaiming Pain

Looking back, I have made many mistakes that I regret deeply. I have learnt the importance of not wasting these painful experiences, but to repent and change my ways.

In my younger days, I made the terrible mistake of practising favouritism and partiality among my children. It was so obvious to others that I favoured my youngest child, Tze Ru, but I could not see it. He was known as "Mama's Boy". I didn't quite know what to do about it; as the saying goes: "We can't tell a drunk man he is drunk."

It is also often said that "it's a squeaky wheel (that) gets the grease".

Being an expressive child, he would make much noise and not give up until he got what he wanted. He was like me. His older brother Tze Lin was like his father — quiet, long-suffering and a man of few words who kept his thoughts and views to himself.

Therefore, unknowingly, I realised I had neglected the needs of my elder son and behaved unfairly towards him by mostly giving in to the demands of my more vocal younger son.

When I came to Christ, I was warned by the Holy Spirit that I have a biblical "Joseph" in Tze Ru, and that my perceived favouritism may have caused a rift in the brothers' relationship.

I realised that I had been better at handling the more outspoken one than the quiet and reserved one; the partiality that I showed one over the other saddened me. The Word of God reminded me that partiality is a sin. Despite how it came across to my sons, I have always loved and cared for both of them in different ways.

Due to this baggage of the past, I am estranged from Tze Lin to this day. I take responsibility for such a dismal state of affairs. I continue to press on to work on myself, believing that God will, one day, let Tze Lin not just see the mother who has hurt and rejected him but to see me as a new creation in Christ by His grace.

This pain that I feel over our strained relationship allows me to minister more authentically to parents who face rejection from their children. When I pray for them, I am able to pray with an inward authenticity because I can empathise and identify with them. I believe that He will make all things beautiful in His time, and that we should not lose heart.

Similarly, it is painful to witness Jing Yin deteriorating before our eyes.

Currently, she has lost her mobility and uses a wheelchair to get around. Occasionally, she also relies on a machine to assist with her breathing. Medically, these losses are an expected part of her deterioration. Instead of giving in to my emotions about her condition, I choose to walk by faith for nothing is too difficult for God, and to stand on His promise of healing when we have accomplished His will (Hebrews 10:35–6).

I used to have many questions about God's economy of healing or lack thereof. On the one hand, I once had a sister-in-law who held down a good job and was very helpful to everyone in the family. However, she had cancer and died in her mid-50s.

On the other hand, God kept my mother alive till the ripe age of 94, although dementia afflicted her for a number of years until there wasn't much of herself left.

Don't get me wrong; I care about my mother and very much hoped that she would be around for as long as possible. However, I still had questions about why many young, economically active and therefore useful persons to society leave us early, while some elderly persons, who are ill and less 'useful' in some sense, still remain on this earth.

To my logical human mind, his economy just doesn't make much utilitarian sense. Over the years, I kept asking God questions like these, but did not receive an answer until the eve of my mother's funeral in December 2019.

That night, God reminded me of the question I had been asking Him all these years. He answered it with another question, asking: "When your husband died, what did you tell your mother?"

I had long forgotten about that exchange but His prompting made me recall that intimate moment in 2006 when, newly widowed and feeling lonesome, I had lamented to my mother in Teochew: "You eat long-long so that you can keep me company." It was an expression in dialect of my desire for her to live as long as possible and be my companion since I had just become a widow then.

Some 13 years later, just the night before my mother's funeral, I heard Him whisper to me: "You don't need Mum anymore. I am taking her Home." His answer was succinct, yet it felt deeply intimate.

Suddenly, everything made sense to me, including the timing of Mum's death. I had left for Sydney in March 2019, and returned prematurely in October. However, I did not return to my home (where I had taken Mum in to live with me after my husband died) as I had to move straight into my son's place to help care for the grandchildren. Mum died peacefully in her sleep two months later in December.

I began to realise that God loves me so much that He had heard and even fulfilled my passing remark to my mother by granting me her companionship for many years after my husband died. I had to take back my words about elderly persons being less 'useful' as Mum had been a fantastic companion to me. When she left, I felt the vacuum in my heart acutely.

I still don't understand why some people die earlier than others, and I don't have to. All I needed was experiencing first-hand the love of God the Father. That quelled all my questions. When we know how much God loves each of us, we can depend on Him rather than seek meaning through our own understanding.

For Jing Yin, He taught me how to pray for her. Instead of merely asking Him to meet her needs, He showed me how I could pray by putting myself in her shoes. This is a form of intercessory prayer where I learnt to identify myself with Jing Yin, her condition and her emotions. Therefore, I do not pray from a distant or aloof position.

For instance, if I am praying for her to have more faith, I don't just tell God to give her more faith. Instead, I pray on her behalf, such as by asking for His forgiveness for being of little faith because I am resentful and angry about the situation I am in, and to ask Him to give me faith to believe Him and His Word.

All these are lessons that God has been teaching me these few years; He desires for me to have (His) compassion, rather than sacrifice (Matthew 9:13).

Prior to moving in with Tze Ru and Jing Yin, I used to have a helper who would prepare my food and clothes, including ensuring that my work and going-out attire matched my accessories, bags and shoes. Now, I do not have anyone to serve me as the helpers at home are preoccupied with caregiving for Jing Yin and the children, as well as other household chores.

One day, as I was rushing to a dinner, I complained to God that I had to iron my own dress and sort out my attire without any help.

He replied: "Don't belly-ache, I want your compassion, and not the sacrifices that you have had to make at home. It's not the 'doing' that's needed of you, it's the 'being'."

I understood that I needed to ask for His compassion for Jing Yin so that I would understand and identify better with the physical challenges that she is facing.

Even though I might think I am so right in my own eyes in the light of my own reasoning and logic, I could be so wrong with God when I do not yield to His Word that asks for me to bear the burdens and weaknesses of those without strength.

Chapter 19

From Cat to Kitten

In order to lead, a good leader must first know how to submit to authority.

In learning to humble myself at home by submitting to my son and daughter-in-law, and cultivating a heart that is not easily offended, I am also empowered to be a better leader at work.

I used to be vocal and rebellious and would go against external authorities, until I realised that I had to submit to external authority because my internal authority, the Word of God, says so.

Every year, we would organise a reception for the Dr Goh Keng Swee Scholarship recipients and its alumni. One year, Dr Goh turned up a bit earlier than the scheduled time to meet the students. Since I had advised our ABS Chairman to come at the scheduled time, he arrived later than Dr Goh. Annoyed at failing to receive and give Dr Goh a proper welcome as he had arrived after him, the Chairman told me off for not advising him to come earlier.

A young lawyer at the reception overheard it and later asked me: "How could you allow him to talk to you like that?" I reassured the young person that the scolding was fine with me as he is my boss and I understood how he must have felt by not being able to be a good host. I should have done better. The old me might have argued back that I would not have known that Dr Goh would arrive early that afternoon. Now I do not take criticisms personally or view them negatively; they are simply opportunities for me to learn and grow.

In areas which we have been tested and which we have overcome — whether it's about submission or something else — we now have the authority to teach and mentor others in the same matter. There was a staff member of mine with whom I was quite close and we even travelled together a number of times. Perhaps due to her familiarity with me, there was an occasion when she did not think twice about publicly berating me at an official meeting.

After the meeting, I called her up immediately. I told her that it was not appropriate for her to come up against her boss publicly as she would be viewed poorly by others for being insubordinate. If she had disagreed with me, she ought to have spoken to me about it in private after the meeting. She had done herself a disservice, I noted, and reminded her not to cross the thin line between professionalism and familiarity.

In the past, like her I would have spoken up. However, I have since learnt to submit to authority and find the opportunity to clarify with my boss. Since I could see my old self in her, I continued to train and nurture her instead of giving up on her.

Over the years, as God transformed me from a fiery, impatient and difficult boss into a meeker and more considerate leader, the various staff who worked under me witnessed the radical change.

ABS' despatch staff, Osman, had worked with me for 27 years since he joined ABS as a young man. When he retired, he had these parting words for me in Malay: "Mrs Ong, *dudu macam harrimau, tapi sakarang macam kucing*." (Mrs Ong, you were a tigress before, but now you have transformed to be like a cat.") I replied in my limited Malay: "*Tak cukup*, Osman, *saya mau tukar serpenti anak kucing*." (Not enough, Osman, I must change till I am like a kitten). I desire to be even meeker and gentler, with God's help, as these qualities are precious to God.

It does not mean being passive or being a pushover. Paradoxically, a meek spirit enables us to yield and align so closely to the purposes and will of God that we gain authority and favour in various life situations.

For instance, over 1,000 people attended an ABS Annual General Meeting dinner in a hotel ballroom in 2019. Everyone was so excited to see each other that they left their tables — after only two courses of food were served — to catch up with one another.

I was the emcee for the event. There I was, on the stage, repeatedly saying, "Ladies and Gentlemen, could I have your attention please", in a bid to get them to sit back down at their respective tables so that we could get on with the next segment of the programme.

After repeating myself thrice over to no avail, I did not know what to do. I could not shout over the microphone as it would have been unpleasant. As I stood there helplessly, I asked God to show me what to do. He told me to sing and so I opened my mouth to sing the one song I was familiar with — "Amazing Grace".

I sang acapella for one stanza of the song and the chatter immediately died down. People turned to look at me and I seized the opportunity of having successfully captured their attention to remind them to sit down. They did so and my job was done. In meekly seeking God in all that I do, I realised that the process could sometimes be unexpectedly out of the box, but the outcome is always effective.

Leadership Succession

After all these years, one important question still remains: Who will lead ABS into a future that is becoming increasingly hard to conceive and prepare for?

It is not due to a lack of trying, or our lack of success in succession planning and training. Internally, the successive Councils and the Chairman banks have continually kept an eye out for the next ABS Director. Each time we try to groom somebody, as we have done three to four times, invariably some trait or requirement for the job would be lacking in the person who had otherwise seemed to have the potential to be the next leader.

Some do not want to take media interviews and appear on TV, while others can do administrative work but do not wish to interact with the regulator MAS. Yet others do not have the banking knowledge or the emotional quotient needed to gain the confidence of both MAS and the banks.

When I became the Director in 1982, ABS needed someone such as myself who had the background of being involved in regulatory and policy work. But the financial sector is evolving and getting more and more digital. By the time I retire, things would have changed to the point that you don't need someone with my experience for the new economy. There would be a need for someone with a different aptitude, wisdom and capacity for that future time.

God sent me to ABS for a time such as this, but to find another Ong Ai Boon to serve in the future decades would neither be possible nor necessary. I believe God will send the right person at the right time with the right background for the job when the time comes. What is needed now is for us to institutionalise and document all our work processes and protocols so that the next leader would have the necessary frameworks from which to learn and thrive.

For me, I hope to work till I am 95, if that is God's will. Friends who have already retired and are enjoying themselves often ask me: "Ai Boon, when are you going to retire?" I answer them with: " Until now, God has not told me that it is time for me to step down."

Forty years on, the work at ABS still energises and excites me. It is very encouraging to hear the younger bankers and MAS officers who work with me telling me that they enjoy the enthusiasm and energy that I exude.

At ABS, we are currently still occupied with major projects in digitalisation, such as PayNow going cross border, sustainable finance and data collection to facilitate the low carbon transition, as well as cyber security and anti-scam issues among others.

My other priority is to be present for my family. As I seek to continually love and serve them, even when it's hard, the home ground becomes another crucible for God to refine me. As I become more Christ-like, I am able to manage ABS as a more enlightened leader and, perhaps, develop the qualities needed to lead ABS into its next phase. Over the years I have seen that the impact I have made through ABS was only a function of how much I allowed God to transform my old self.

Through the years, ABS has become a trusted institution in Singapore's financial landscape, and has received its fair share of recognition and accolades. Just as it has quietly supported the making of Singapore as a global financial centre, it remains ready and confident in helping the city-state flourish further, regardless of what the future holds.

When the time comes for the baton to be passed, I believe the next Director who helms ABS will possess the intellectual and emotional competence and strength of character needed to grow the trust that the Association has forged over the years. I also hope that he or she might find this documentation of a small slice of its history to be a useful guide.

It was His grace that has led me and ABS thus far, and grace will follow us still.

Epilogue

I was in the car with my late husband, who was driving me to an appointment. It seemed to be yet another mundane and routine appointment so there wasn't any special conversation between us.

Soon, we arrived at a row of shophouses and I alighted. I walked towards a shophouse that had a signboard above it which read: "EXECUTION HOUSE". I knew I was going for an "appointment to die" yet I didn't feel a sense of foreboding or dread. It was as if I was going for my usual hair or nail appointment. I casually entered the shophouse and went straight up to the registration counter.

Promptly, I told the nurse at the reception: "I am Ong Ai Boon."

"It's the band on your right wrist that I need," came her terse reply.

I glanced at my wrist and, to my surprise, I saw that indeed I had a band that looked like a hospital identification tag. I had not noticed it before.

"How do I know, I have not died before!" I immediately retorted. In my state of annoyance, sharp claws, like those of a cat, came out of my hands, as if ready to strike reflexively.

The nurse checked the register and told me to wait for my name to be called. I decided to wait outside the shophouse.

As I stepped out, I turned right and walked along an inner, unpaved road. After a short walk, I sat down on the parapet next to a drain.

As I did so, a large bramble bush with small fairies flying about — similar to those seen in the Shakespearean play "A Midsummer's Night Dream" — appeared in front of me. The fairies were talking among themselves and I overheard them saying; "This Ai Boon … she is very good for small groups and one-to-one ministry."

I nodded in agreement, smiled to myself and muttered: "Ya! What they say is true. I am good with small group ministry and one-to-one sharing."

Then, I realised that it was getting dark, and I did not want to miss my appointment. As I got up, the bramble bush vanished and I walked quickly back to the shophouse. On the way back, I saw a group of my church friends sitting around a table having dinner in a restaurant but reminded myself not to stop to talk as I did not want to be late for the appointment.

Hurriedly, I walked on and checked in at the registration counter again when I arrived. The nurse looked through the registration book again, then looked up at me and said: "Oh! Your appointment has been cancelled."

"I see, okay," I replied, while thinking to myself, "I hope my husband is still in the carpark and able to give me a lift back home." When I went out of the shophouse and turned left towards the carpark, it was already dark.

In the carpark, I saw my husband in a green Volvo sitting at the driver's seat, talking to a friend who was next to him. Upon opening the back seat door, a blast of cold air from the air-con within hit my face. I told my husband that my appointment was cancelled and asked if he could send me home. He nodded. As I got into the back seat, he drove off.

I woke up from this vivid dream, which I had sometime in August 2021, without feeling any fear or apprehension. Instead, I was fascinated by its detail and divine implication on the rest of my life.

What was clear to me, or at least what felt very palpable, was that I could have died in my sleep that night. I was 74 years old at that time. In the dream, I had an imminent appointment to die, and even saw my late husband who had crossed over to the other side in 2006. Yet in the end, my appointment with Death was cancelled.

What happened in between that gave me an extended lease on life?

To me, I felt the key lay in how I had acknowledged the fairies' remarks that I was gifted in certain aspects of ministry and, in so doing, I was agreeable to continue with it. It seemed to me that my time on earth was not yet up because there is still a prophetic agenda for me. I am making myself available for the work to be done, by His grace, be it at home or in the office.

Since then, I have continued to receive requests to speak in small groups in offices, homes and churches to teach and encourage believers to grow in their faith. Every week, I also continue to lead at least three different groups of people — office fellowship on Mondays, ladies' fellowship on Thursdays and the women's group from my church on Fridays. I rarely turn down invitations to speak and minister, even before this dream occurred. However, the dream further endorsed and affirmed this ministry of mine, and gives me the added motivation to continue doing it in my golden years. My heart's desire is to hear God say to me when I meet Him in heaven: "Well done, my good and faithful servant!"

My one-to-one ministry at home is also key in this new season.

My daughter-in-law has been physically deteriorating from Motor Neurone Disease over the past few years. We pray together often, and in our helplessness, we depend more and more on God.

Even in my advanced age, I struggle with having to submit to my son's and daughter-in-law's authority and instruction while living under their roof. It is ever more important for me to not take offence at perceived slights and to bear the fruit of the Spirit if my earnest desire is for them to know God deeply. For it is through people around them, like myself, that they may see and encounter the love and nature of God. I also wait for God's promise — that the symptoms that Jing Yin now has will go away — to come to pass.

As for my work with ABS, I find that my effectiveness and success at work grows in tandem with my own transformation in character and maturity as I grow in my walk with God.

When I first joined the Association some 40 years ago, I was handed a list of seven KPIs as a benchmark for what was expected of the new permanent secretariat of the Association.

Over the years, I have largely forgotten about those targets, until they resurfaced during the research process for this book. Looking at them again after four decades, I was struck by how, without deliberate planning on my part to meet those objectives, the Association has achieved them, and I dare say with flying colours. Out of the seven boxes, all have been ticked but one — research and development — the only area the Association did not delve into as I thought the banks were better resourced for this.

☑ 1. Effective government relations

☑ 2. Effective member relations

☑ 3. Effective association leadership

☑ 4. Effective information/data exchange and uniform operating procedures and standards

☑ 5. Better developed human assets and highly effective staff for the banking community

☑ 6. Enhancement of banking services through promotion, development and improvement, if necessary, of infrastructure for a modern banking centre in association with the appropriate authorities

☐ 7. Research and development

It's not me. It is clear to me that none of these — whether the greatest achievements or biggest milestones of my life — was of my own doing. Each and every good thing in my life has been achieved by the grace of God.

God took the lowest moments of my life — the valleys — and not only levelled them up, but redeemed them to become mountaintop experiences.

My husband wanting to walk out on our marriage was the best wake-up call of my life. When I began to yield to God's guidance in transforming myself, I never thought I would see the day when my husband would gift me with 100 red roses on my 55th birthday some two decades later with a note that said: "Totally in love with you, Hubby." My mother was a demure Teochew woman who was often critical of my loud and brash demeanour. Her common refrain to me was: "If only you were more like me." I never thought I would see the day when she prayed and told God: "Lord, I want to be like my daughter."

I also never thought I would see the day when one of the ABS staff (who had worked with me for 27 years) remarked to me when he retired: "Mrs Ong, *dudu macam harrimau, tapi sakarang macam kuching.*" (Mrs Ong, you were a tigress before, but now you have been transformed to be like a cat.)

My work in ABS is God's calling and He will give me the grace to do what is expected of me. His grace lifted me above my limitations. My 40 years of helming ABS have turned out far better than I could have imagined. He has done it and will continue to do it, even as I set my hope in Him. It's not me, but His ever-sufficient grace that carries me forth, from my past and present, into the future.

Reflections from My Son

By Ong Tze Ru

The years 1982 and 1983 marked the start of two separate developments in my life, both of which would later turn out to be interlinked and end up critically shaping my life.

I was just six years old in 1982 when I first climbed the staircase that led to the mezzanine-level premises of the first ABS office at PIL Building along Cecil Street to visit my mother, Ai Boon, in her office. Little did I realise then how ABS would come to shape my life. For the next 40 years I, too, would have my own 'ABS experience' through my interactions with my mother and many of her staff.

Over the decades, I visited the ABS office fairly frequently and became familiar with her entire team, some of whom prayed for me along with my mother, and who have become as close to me as family. Even at home, I would still be subject to the 'ABS treatment' as I used to overhear my mother's work discussions with my father, her staff and work associates. I became exposed to the names of local and foreign institutions and their senior management along with key financial sector projects.

It was through all these influences that I myself chose a career path in the banking industry. Thus, ABS holds a special place in my heart and played an important part in my formative years.

In 1983, my mother became a Christian. And not just an ordinary Christian, but one that was 'born again' and totally set on fire with tremendous passion for Christ. As soon as she woke up in the morning, she would play and sing along to the then popular and wonderfully composed Maranatha Christian worship songs. She played them so much that to this day I, too, can sing along to any of those 80s and 90s worship songs perfectly from memory. That year, she taught me how to pray and exposed me to the charismatic Christian movement.

She also showed me that when we have The Light in our lives, we need not be afraid of being honest and open about our fears and shortcomings. In fact, the act of doing so becomes our very strength in Christ.

Mum and I have a very similar personality. I inherited a bad temper as a chip off the old block, but she has also taught me so much about being an overcomer in Christ.

What was most crucial was how the Christian and ABS worlds were so closely intertwined in my mother's life — in a good way and to much benefit. This book's narrative wonderfully weaves through and alternates between descriptions of the role of ABS in the development of Singapore's financial sector, and Mum's own personal journey. It mirrors how she has lived out her personal, professional and Christian lives in an integrated way — they really are one and the same.

My mother finds purpose and fulfilment in her work at ABS because its many contributions to the development of the financial sector not only benefit the country, but have had a direct and positive impact on the daily lives of all Singaporeans. But it doesn't just stop there. Her work (and workplace) is also a platform that is used to minister, help and reach out to others. She allows God to use the furnace of difficulties and struggles at work to shape, mould and refine her character.

Most importantly, her relationship with God gets strengthened with each obstacle she overcomes. She prays incessantly and continually goes to the Bible to hear from Him. Funnily, in this entire process, she has actually had a lot of fun. That is because what excites her most of all is to see the Hand of God moving from start to finish, transforming what looked to be an awful beginning into a beautiful outcome.

Maybe you are facing your own challenges at your workplace, within your family or in your relationships. You will probably be able to identify with many of the situations that she presents in this book — the circumstances may be different, but the difficulties are the same. Her experiences will give you some insight and ideas as to how you, too, can find a way to overcome your own obstacles.

This book cites many of her experiences relating to her work in the financial sector, but they are, in fact, just the tip of the iceberg of the totality of her experiences. Over the past many decades, she has also been involved in counselling and mentoring countless persons outside of the work setting. Marriages have been saved and parent-child relationships restored. There is more than enough material and testimonies for a second book to be written!

But again, her approach in these instances is the same as it has been for her workplace — extending copious amounts of love and grace through Christ, being led by the wisdom of the Holy Spirit to get to the root of the issue, and making sure her words and actions are grounded in the Word of God.

It has now been four years since my wife, Jing Yin, has been diagnosed with Motor Neurone Disease, which is a devastating neurological condition. Yet, ever since the initial diagnosis in July 2019, Mum has been an absolute pillar of strength because of her relationship with God. Her faith is ever steadfast and she has lifted up our spirits on countless occasions.

As I was reviewing this book prior to writing this reflection, I was facing a particularly difficult time with Jing Yin's deteriorating physical condition. However, as I read through this book, I was, firstly, reminded about how my family and I have been directly blessed by Mum's walk with God in both her workplace and at home.

Secondly, I was also inspired to follow her example to overcome, and indeed, two weeks later, Jing Yin and I had a critical spiritual and emotional breakthrough to a part-medical, part-psychological issue that had been plaguing Jing Yin for several months.

I am certain that you will be blessed (and entertained!) as you read through this book. It is the story of an ordinary woman with ordinary intelligence and talents being a part of extraordinary achievements simply because she puts Christ front and centre of everything and anything that she does. Follow these same principles and I guarantee that you, too, will have your own extraordinary stories to tell.

Acknowledgements

All royalties from the sale of this book will be donated to Christian ministries that further the work of Christ until His return.

Looking back on the nearly eight decades I have been in this world, I can see God's hand in weaving the tapestry of my life. I thank and praise Him for turning me from earthly ambitions to spiritual pursuits, which have, in turn, overflowed to much fruitfulness in this world. I am grateful for the people the Lord has sent my way who have made a real difference in my life — among whom are many who have upheld me in their prayers through the years. The following is hardly a complete list of the people I need to thank.

I owe a lifelong debt of gratitude and love to my mother, two brothers and three sisters, my late husband, two sons and daughter, and the rest of our families, who have seen the best and worst of me. They have been generous to let me pour myself into my work and ministries, and have been patient and long-suffering through my transformation journey.

The ABS staff members are my Ace Team — everything that the Association has achieved would not be possible without you. Thanks for enduring this tough boss — your dedication and hard work are always appreciated. To Shimah and Linda, thank you for sticking with me through the good, bad and ugly from the start.

To all 14 ABS Chairmen — those from the Big Four to the present three local banks — with whom I have had the pleasure of working, as well as the many Council members through the years, your generous contributions of leadership, guidance and experience have been critical to the Association's success. I am grateful for the many professional and personal insights I have gleaned from my time with you.

The work of ABS stands on the commitment and contributions of the many members of the ABS committees and taskforces. Thanks for answering the call to serve and for unquestioningly taking many of my calls for help.

My bosses and colleagues at MAS gave me an invaluable foundation for my subsequent station at ABS. From imbibing Singapore's vision to be an international financial centre to working the nuts and bolts of policymaking, those 10 years at MAS could not have been a more apt preparation for the next 40 years (and more) when I continued to work with many of you in the very same building. Thanks for the close partnership with ABS that has been nurtured over the years. Having worked together on so many projects, it is gratifying to see how the industry has flourished over the past 50 years.

It was an ASEAN Banking Conference that opened my eyes to the potential of ABS and, since then, the work and relationships shared with my counterparts in the region, through the ASEAN Bankers Association, have been rich and rewarding. I am most grateful for your partnership, hospitality and fellowship.

This book owes its existence to many people, and has been an opportunity to reconnect with old friends and meet new ones.

Credit for the book's genesis goes to Sopnendu and Navin, who sprang the idea on me in November 2021 and did not let me give up on it. Thanks for welcoming this digital dinosaur into your Fintech world. It was exhilarating and eye-opening to be involved in organising the first SFF and it is most gratifying to see SFF grow to become the world's largest, most influential and successful global platform for FinTech.

To Peter Heng, Freddy Orchard, Bryan Lee, Jeffrey Ong and Karen Ng — thanks for journeying with me on this project and for lending your knowledge, skills and time to conceptualise and re-conceptualise the project, conduct research, chase up old contacts, articulate my thoughts on paper, review drafts and many other things that are too numerous to list. Most importantly, thanks for all the encouragement and reassurance you gave me. Thanks for listening to my woes, and for suggestions around roadblocks through this arduous project that has brought me much stress and many sleepless nights.

I first met Janice Tai in 2020 when she interviewed me for a *Salt&Light* article. When I realised that my faith had to be integral to the book, I thought of her and I am so glad she (and her bosses) agreed to take up this project. God could not have sent me a more appropriate writer. I am grateful for Janice's gentle and calm spirit, yet firm hand, that was key in gathering together my many ramblings and turning it into a coherent story of God's work in and through me, as well as presenting it in a most readable and engaging manner. I am also grateful to Juleen Shaw, the Managing Editor of *Salt&Light*, for polishing up the manuscript.

To Sue-Ann, Jacqueline and the rest of the Nutgraf team — thanks for your patience and professionalism in writing the first version of the book.

To Hong Koon, Lai Ann and the team at World Scientific, thanks for accommodating the many changes and for getting the book ready in time for its publication.

About the Authors

ONG-ANG AI BOON is the Director of The Association of Banks in Singapore (ABS). She was appointed in 1982 and has since been leading ABS with her extensive regulatory and operational experience in the banking industry.

Ai Boon started her career in banking in 1969 at Chung Khiaw Bank. Prior to joining ABS, she was with the Monetary Authority of Singapore (MAS) from 1971 till 1981 where she held several key positions.

The Association represents the interests of the banking industry (155 local and foreign banks) and, among other functions, works to establish a sound banking structure in Singapore in collaboration and consultation with MAS and other government bodies.

Ai Boon had an interesting encounter with Christ and was born again in 1983 while seeking the meaning of life. She is an Advisory Elder at City Missions Church. She is also a regular speaker at Christian conferences, meetings and cell groups, sharing authentically about how she lives out her faith both in the workplace and at home.

JANICE TAI is a Senior Writer with faith-based platform *Salt&Light*, which uses digital media for outreach and discipleship. She was formerly a Social Affairs Correspondent at Singapore's national newspaper *The Straits Times* for almost a decade. Her multimedia projects and feature articles have been recognised in both local and international news awards. She is also an author and editor of several books.